Boris Becker's
WIMBLEDON

Boris Becker's
WIMBLEDON

with Chris Bowers

BLINK
bringing you closer

Published by Blink Publishing
107-109 The Plaza,
535 King's Road,
Chelsea Harbour,
London, SW10 0SZ

www.blinkpublishing.co.uk

facebook.com/blinkpublishing
twitter.com/blinkpublishing

978-1-910536-08-7

A CIP catalogue of this book is available from the British Library.

Design by Blink Publishing

Printed and bound by Interak, Poland

1 3 5 7 9 10 8 6 4 2

Papers used by Blink Publishing are natural, recyclable products made from wood grown in sustainable forests. The manufacturing processes conform to the environmental regulations of the country of origin.

Blink Publishing is an imprint of the Bonnier Publishing Group
www.bonnierpublishing.co.uk

To the worldwide Becker family, in particular:

Noah, Elias, Anna and Amadeus

*and in loving memory of my late father Karl-Heinz,
who encouraged me to be the man I am today,
and who I very much sound like these days when
I talk to my own children!*

Contents

Acknowledgements

A book like this doesn't just happen because I want it to happen. It takes the efforts of a number of people, and I am grateful to various individuals for contributions big and small. They include John Blake, Nick Brown, Craig Gabriel, Brian Holmes, Chris Lewis and Audrey Snell. I'm particularly indebted to Chris Bowers who found my voice in both English and German, to my agent Adrian Sington, and to Joel Simons and Clare Tillyer from Blink Publishing. Most of all, my love and gratitude go to my wife Lilly – I wouldn't be living in Wimbledon without her, and she has helped me make Wimbledon into my home.

Boris Becker
June 2015

Foreword

By Novak Djokovic

Welcome to *Boris Becker's Wimbledon*! Boris welcomed me to his Wimbledon in the summer of 2014, during our first year working together as player and coach. The stories of how he showed me 'his city' and how my wife Jelena and I dropped in one night while we were out walking the dog are told in chapter 9, and testify to the fact that Wimbledon is not just a tennis tournament for Boris but is very much his home, a home I could profit from in the pursuit of my second Wimbledon title.

But my gratitude to Boris goes back much further than that.

I wasn't even born when Boris won his first Wimbledon title, and he won his last title when I was two and hadn't discovered tennis. When I took my first steps on a tennis court at the age of five, I was mainly watching Sampras and Agassi.

But Boris did influence my tennis game indirectly. I have this one very important recollection from my past about Boris.

When I was 12 years old, I had to leave my country to look for better facilities and conditions for training. My parents and my coach, Jelena Genčić, thought that Niki Pilić's academy in Munich would be the best place for me at that time. Niki generally didn't work with kids until they were at least 14, but he and his wife were kind enough to allow me to be there even though I was a couple of years younger than the other kids attending his academy.

I remember well my first day there. I was both excited and anxious. It had not been easy to leave my brothers and parents and be in a foreign country, but I knew I had to do it if I wanted to reach my dream of becoming the best tennis player in the world. I remember how everything seemed strange and new, exciting and scary at the same time. I was passing by the hallway to get to the indoor training facilities, and on the wall I saw photos of Niki and Boris Becker, the greatest male tennis champion that Germany ever had. And he played on the same tennis courts where I was about to spend months and months away from my family!

That made my blood rush so fast through my body, I was so motivated to get on court and show the world that I can do it, that I can be a champion too! It was a really sensational feeling. Just a few days earlier, I had been in Serbia, a war-torn country with no facilities or means to cultivate a tennis professional, let alone a tennis champion. It really felt like confirmation that I was in the right place.

Even though I didn't look at Boris as my idol, I admired his ability to become a Wimbledon champion at such a young age, to defy the odds, to be such an aggressive and furious player on court, to always fight till the end. Niki was my coach, and a person who helped me lift my game to a higher level, but Boris was also indirectly there, confirming to me that it was the right place for me to be. I can only imagine how many other kids he has inspired both directly and indirectly – just by being the champion he is – to be better people and better athletes.

It's really a privilege to have him today in my box as my coach and a person I look to for eye contact in the tough moments. I feel like the sky's the limit when our two minds collide, and I'm excited to see where the future will lead us.

This book tells you about the moments that shaped him and allowed him to be the inspiration he was to me and to others. I hope you enjoy it.

ROLEX

THE CHAMPIONSHIPS
WIMBLEDON
THE CHAMPIONSHIPS

Slazenger
ROBINSONS

COURT No.19
K. Schmiedlova SVK 1 15
M. Gordon USA 0 30

NO.1 COURT
PREVIOUS SETS

THE CHAMPIONSHIPS
WIMBLEDON

Introduction

THE CHAMPIONSHIPS
WIMBLEDON

'Wimbledon, please,' I say to the taxi driver after clearing customs at London Heathrow Airport.

The driver recognises me. 'Yes sir,' he says, with a nod that seems to imply: where else would Boris Becker want to go but Wimbledon? But I'm not going to the All England Lawn Tennis Club. I'm going home. Yes, home today is Wimbledon, where my wife Lilly, my son Amadeus and I live.

To some people this may seem like a dream. A small-town boy from the rural south of Germany wins Wimbledon at 17 and ends up living within walking distance of the scene of his biggest triumph. It's not quite like that. When I finished my playing career in 1999, I moved to Zurich after periods living in Monaco and Munich. I was still based in Zurich when I met Lilly, who's Dutch but was living in Miami at the time. When Amadeus was on the way, we knew we had to settle down somewhere, but where? By then, a fixed part of my year was based around Wimbledon, because from 2002 the BBC had included me as part of their Wimbledon commentary team. So London seemed an obvious choice (the mayor was even called Boris!), and we decided Wimbledon, with its village feel, was the place we wanted to raise our family.

Above: **I first won Wimbledon as *a* 17-year-old in 1985.**

So Wimbledon became my home, and it feels like home in many senses of the word. Two of my four children were born in London, we speak English at home, I have a business in the city of London, and I'm a member of my local tennis club (the All England Lawn Tennis and Croquet Club) even though I don't play much these days. I'm a member thanks to having won their tournament, which saved me a 20-year spell on the club's waiting list. More importantly, I love Wimbledon as a village, and while things may change, at the moment I'd be happy to spend the rest of my life with Wimbledon as home.

A lot has been written about me. That's inevitable, it comes with the territory, and I accept it as part of the deal that has

Right: **The crowds gather for another blockbuster match on Centre Court.**

ANDY!

given me such a good life. But because so many things that are not true have been written by so many people, and because Wimbledon is so special to me, I feel it's my right – if not my obligation or my duty – to explain from my perspective what Wimbledon is, what Wimbledon meant and what Wimbledon will be for me in the future.

This book is therefore a homage to Wimbledon. It is not without a little criticism along the way, but it is intended to be an affectionate reflection on my relationship with Wimbledon, and perhaps a little of Wimbledon's relationship with me. And it's not just a journalistic coincidence that it comes out at the time of the 30th anniversary of my first Wimbledon title when I was just 17. I am writing it now because I feel I have come full circle.

Since becoming the head coach to Novak Djokovic, I have returned to the Wimbledon locker room. The place that was my home away from home for so long. When Novak approached me at the end of 2013, many people questioned whether I could offer him enough to justify being the coach to one of the best players in the world. They were entitled to question whether I was the right man, but some of that debate strayed into the realms of questioning whether I really knew much about tennis, which is a bit crazy as well as insulting. The fact that, on my first visit to Wimbledon as the coach to a top-class player, he emerged with the trophy has largely silenced the doubters.

***Left:* I became Novak's coach at the end of 2013. Six months later he walked off Centre Court with the Men's Singles Title trophy.**

I think those critics now see that tennis in general and Wimbledon in particular is part of my DNA. When you leave so much of your soul out there as a player, there is always something you can offer. Even though it is more than 15 years since I quit as a player, I still talk about myself as a player in the present tense, because I still have the player's mentality. That's why I'm so comfortable back in the locker room, why I completely understand the struggles of Novak and others – after all, I had the same struggles. It feels like the more I talk about it the more it comes back. It was so much part of my life, and I think it always will be.

I hope, therefore, that this book is not just a trip down the memory lane of my Wimbledon and other experiences, but a look back at how tennis has developed over the past 30 years. In some ways tennis is better now, but in other ways it isn't. I have my opinions, and I don't shy away from sharing them. But sometimes all I will leave you with is material to discuss in the tennis club bar after a game, or over a drink with friends. There's a lot to be debated in tennis on issues where there are two or three legitimate ways to go.

I was 17 when I first won Wimbledon. I'm 47 now. In the intervening years, the boy who played on aggressive instinct has become the man caring for an international patchwork family; the cheeky lad who knew no fear has become the celebrity wary of those who forever look to create the next Becker headline. And Wimbledon has evolved too – from the lovable but 'father knows best' tournament it was in the 1980s to the superb branded event it is today, a spectacle that has managed to keep its distinct character while constantly modernising. I'm proud that so much of my growing up has happened at Wimbledon, and I'm proud to be a part of its glorious history.

Boris Becker,
June 2015

***Right:* My life has been intertwined with the greatest Grand Slam of them all: Wimbledon.**

Chapter 1

First time on grass, first time at Wimbledon

'You're not going to break an egg with that serve.'

We live today in a world of social media. Everything we do is reported online, perhaps because we post it or somebody else does it for us. Tennis is a very popular sport, so it attracts a lot of interest in social and world media. In addition, the top guys make a lot of money, and there are a lot of sharks out there looking for the next big thing. So if you get a 15-year-old or 16-year-old starting to win a few matches at a Grand Slam tournament, it gets blown completely out of proportion. And the likelihood is that the player would start to believe the hype, and that would affect their performance.

I say this because people often ask whether a 17-year-old could win Wimbledon now. My answer is: yes, of course, but it's highly unlikely to happen. Today's wisdom has it that tennis has become more physical, and therefore you can't win a Grand Slam tournament until you're at least 20. I don't believe that – I think a 17-year-old could easily be physically capable of winning a major, but would they have the maturity to handle the whole circus that would accompany them? That's the question. When I was 17 we were more sheltered. The media was still interested in me, just as it was interested in Mats Wilander winning the French at 17 in 1982, and Michael Chang winning the French at 17 in 1989. But it wasn't such big news – big news then was that someone had been killed, or there was an earthquake or a revolution somewhere. These days anything

Right: **I was the youngest-ever Grand Slam champion when I picked up the Wimbledon trophy in 1985.**

Michael Chang (*below, right*) defeated my great rival Stefan Edberg at the 1989 French Open to take my crown as the youngest-ever Grand Slam champion. I'd previously taken it from Mats Wilander (*below*).

that would give the media a higher rating or higher readership justifies a headline, with the result that minor stories create headlines, irrespective of their importance, or lack of it.

If I was 17 now, I would be capable of winning Wimbledon, but a lot more would be asked of my maturity. The age of mobile phones, texting, social media and all the other aspects of the internet means that the protection I was given when I tapped into the raw power that saw me take the title in 1985 could never have worked today.

My manager Ion Ţiriac and my coach Günther Bosch kept me in a bubble during that year's Wimbledon. I was aware of how attitudes towards me were changing in the locker room, but I was blissfully unaware of any fuss happening outside. As I worked my way through the draw, there were more requests for interviews. It wasn't just that a 17-year-old was in the second week, I was winning matches I should have lost – I had two highly unlikely five-set victories in the third and fourth rounds, and in one of them I even threw in the towel, but neither my opponent nor the umpire saw it before I had the chance to change my mind. Ţiriac kept most of the interview requests at bay, which allowed me to keep my focus. My family even kept from me the fact that my grandfather had died on the eve of the championships, because I loved him so much and they knew the news would affect me. You just couldn't do that now – I'd

Right: **My love affair with Wimbledon began in 1976 after I saw Björn Borg win the first of five Wimbledon Championships.**

PREVIOUS SETS
SETS GAMES POINTS
B.BORG

get a text about it, or it would leak out through Facebook or Twitter.

Such are the changes that have taken place over the past 30 years. As teenagers, my friends and I didn't feel we were living in prehistoric times – we may not have had email, mobiles or even faxes, but we had telephones in every home. We also had television, the cultural development that frightened our parents and made them think we'd all end up with square eyes. And it was thanks to television that my love affair with Wimbledon began.

I started playing tennis at about three, and at six I won my first tournament. So I was into tennis early, but in those days there was virtually no tennis on German television. We only had three channels – two national ones and a regional 'third programme'. Football had its regular slot on Saturdays and in midweek, but tennis was hardly on TV at all. And then one day a tournament appeared: Wimbledon. The first Wimbledon I remember was when I was eight, and it was Björn Borg winning the first of his five titles. That was 1976, and it was the first time the term 'Wimbledon' entered my consciousness.

It was fascinating to me because they were playing on grass. Some of my courts were green with white lines – the indoor courts of TC Blau-Weiss Leimen (literally the 'Blue & White Tennis Club of Leimen'), which were on a carpet. That's where we played in the winter months, while in the summer we played on red clay. My father was an architect, in fact he designed the buildings for Blau-Weiss Leimen, as well as the national training centre next to the club which players like Steffi Graf and Anke Huber have used over the years. And what do people like him do with their kids at weekends? They go to the tennis club, so I learned to play. My sister Sabine – who's four years older than me – became my first tennis coach.

I've been back to the TC Blau-Weiss a few times since. Nothing has changed; it's still exactly the same. I don't really mind that – it's a small clay court club that serves its purpose. I feel it was an important part of my life, it gave me a great foundation away from the glitz and glamour, and it can happily remain the same. What I find sad is the fact that the national tennis centre next door hasn't changed; it even has the same coaches that were there 25 years ago. That shows where the DTB, the German tennis federation, is going wrong. We're not moving with the times, the understanding about how professional tennis is now played hasn't arrived in Germany yet.

If you've followed my career, you'll know the name 'Leimen', but this isn't some regional metropolis. Leimen is a sleepy, semi-industrial town, and when I was growing up it had less than 20,000 inhabitants. The nearest centre is Heidelberg, seven kilometres away, or a 20-minute bus ride. I'd go there with my friends on a Saturday night or with my mother if I needed some clothes. For this size of town there could easily have been no tennis centre at all, or perhaps just a small club with two or

***Left:* I began playing tennis at the age of three and won my first tournament at six.**

three clay courts that you could use for about seven months of the year until the first frosts came. So to have a club with indoor courts next door was a stroke of luck for me.

Being a tennis fan, Wimbledon as the only televised tournament was very important, and my fascination with grass grew with it. Just to practise on it once, or play a match on it once, became one of my goals. There was only one grass court in the whole of Germany, in Grünwald, a suburb of Munich, but it was privately owned by a family so no-one could play there.

In retrospect, the work I did in the winter on the indoor courts laid the foundations for my game on grass. The indoor surface was a pile carpet; you play on it wearing tennis shoes that have totally flat soles, and it was very quick. The game you have to play on that kind of carpet is very similar to the game played on grass at that time – you had to serve and volley, the return was very important, and basically the first shot is the one that counts. The bounce was fairly low, and there weren't many long rallies. Grass is softer than carpet, but the movement and playing style were very similar. So although I had no idea what playing on grass was like, what I watched on TV from Wimbledon was very much the same game I played indoors in Leimen.

The one thing they didn't seem to do at Wimbledon was dive, and I did dive. No-one taught me, I just did it. You had to do it well, because on a carpet court you could easily burn your knees. I did it very innocently. I guess people looked at me and saw a 'never say die' attitude, but I wasn't aware of that. It was just a quick and instinctive reaction on my part – if I couldn't get to the ball using my feet, I instinctively dived. It wasn't something I thought about, though obviously it gives you great satisfaction afterwards. The roll after the dive was also something I just developed – I played a lot of football, I was a good goalkeeper, so the roll came very naturally to me. My coach at the time, Boris Breskvar, later introduced tennis practice with soft mats, so people could learn to dive like me, but he never did that when I was learning.

Breskvar was an interesting character, and there are echoes of him in my life today coaching Novak Djokovic. He came from Slovenia, which was then part of Yugoslavia, and he had a passion for tennis. He later wrote a book about the way he coached, which a lot of national tennis associations could learn from today. He was more interested in getting the mentality right than focusing on strokes. He had a passion for winning and for competing, whether it was tennis, football, basketball or some other sport. It wasn't about the perfect forehand but about the physical and mental sides, and that made a difference in my professional life. He was all for playing eight hours a day, just to compete. The atmosphere in his training centres in the afternoon was great – there were lots of people playing, there was action, there was noise; it wasn't just hitting the ball, it was loud, it was passionate, and everyone loved it and wanted to come back the next day.

***Right:* The one thing they didn't seem to do at Wimbledon was dive...**

FILA

ellesse

I think the passion that Breskvar had is the reason why so many ex-Yugoslavians are so good at sports. There's a great passion for sport, understanding of sport, in that part of Europe – and it extends to Bulgaria and Romania too. Physically they're all great athletes, and they're all fighters – Goran Ivanišević was a fighter, Marin Čilić is a fighter. And I don't think it's a coincidence that my first real coach was an ex-Yugoslav and the player I'm coaching today is ex-Yugoslav. I'm comfortable with the mentality.

The biggest individual thing Breskvar did for me was to completely remodel my serve. One weekend, I must have been 10 or 11, he was really unhappy with my serve, and he said 'You're not going to break an egg with the serve you have,' so we spent the weekend completely remodelling it. By Monday I couldn't serve at all, but he told me to stick with it. I then figured out myself which position I had to adopt, what body shape, what rhythm, but in the early days it needed a lot of thought before I tossed the ball. It was that preparation and thinking time that led to the rocking motion that my serve became known for, and which people like Mansour Bahrami and Novak Djokovic imitate when they do their tennis player impressions. It came about by my thinking whether I was in the right place, and whether my feet and shoulders were right – there was a lot to think about until it became second nature.

***Left:* My coach Boris Breskvar instructed me to go back to basics with my serve. It was perhaps one of the most important pieces of advice I received during my career.**

I don't need to say how important that weekend of remodelling was to my tennis career. My serve was the cornerstone of my game, and when it was working well, the rest of my game was on. At the end of 2014, at a press conference to announce the formation of a new five-man ATP advisory committee, John McEnroe said the three best serves in the history of tennis were mine, Goran's and Pete Sampras's. I think I broke a few eggs with the serve Boris Breskvar taught me.

My ambition to play on grass – if only just once – was realised when I was 14, and I took to it like a duck to water. I loved it! Yes, there were bad bounces, probably a lot more then than there are now. They say you have to be prepared for every fifth ball to do something strange – the courts I played on were so bad it was more like every third ball, and on some courts you never got the same bounce twice. But people don't understand that a lot on grass has to do with your movement. That's the key. The players who do well at Wimbledon obviously have to serve and return well, but above all they have to move well. And from the moment I first played on grass I felt comfortable moving on the surface.

The first time I played on grass was at a junior tournament in 1982 in Thames Ditton, a private club on the south-western edge of London. I was the best junior in Germany (in indoor tournaments I was already the men's national champion), so I travelled with other top juniors, people like Tore Meinecke, Christian Schmidt, Eric Jelen and Charly Steeb, some of whom went on to have good professional careers. We weren't staying in hotels, it was the YMCA or a Bed & Breakfast, but it felt cool because we were on tour as tennis players. I was very excited about playing on grass, I'd seen so many Wimbledon finals, I'd heard so many stories about it and I was keen to find out what it was like to play on.

We practised for a short time the day before our first matches, and I immediately fell in love with grass. From my first few steps on the court, it felt as if it was the only thing I'd done all my life. I never slid much on any surface, I liked to plant my feet firmly and get a good footing before hitting my shots, and that works well on grass. I had quite muscular legs, I could bend down and get low without crumbling – that's also a secret on grass.

I won my first round, and that night I remember being so excited having played my first match on grass. I think I reached the semis in that tournament.

It wasn't my first time in London. That came when I was 10, when the best under-12s from Germany (Udo Riglewski and I) played against the best under-12s from Great Britain (Richard Whichello and Jason Goodall). Don't ask me about the result – the English don't like being reminded about defeats to Germany! It was my first-ever plane trip, from Frankfurt to London Heathrow. I don't remember much about London because we stayed in a cheap hotel and spent all the time playing tennis, but I do remember flying over the city and thinking how big it was, certainly compared with what I was used to.

My first time through the gates of Wimbledon came in 1983, when I played the junior tournament. I was 15, and we were staying in a Bed & Breakfast somewhere in London. The German national tennis squad had a bus, and all the juniors travelled in the bus to the ground, or we may even have taken the train part of the way. As I walked through the gates, I was struck by how green it was, and so white. I walked the grounds, taking in the flowers and the foliage on Centre Court. I thought it was so quiet – you have 100,000-or-so people around you, but it was still so quiet. Back in the day you had no mobile phones and no other technical gadgets, so it was nothing like now – it was almost an eerie feeling.

Even at 15 I was playing in the under-18s because I was good enough. But there was one guy who dominated the whole year, and I happened to draw him in the first round. I wasn't seeded as I wasn't playing that many tournaments (I was still at school), and this kid, Stefan Edberg, was 22 months older than me. I'd played him before but never beaten him – two years is a big age gap when you're 15 and 17 – and he came to Wimbledon having just won the French Open junior title. He didn't like having to face me, and I didn't like having to face him, but 6-4, 6-4 later I was out and he went on to win the tournament. He went on to win all four junior Grand Slams that year, the only time that's ever been done, so in retrospect it wasn't a bad defeat.

As a first-round loser, I was only at Wimbledon for two or three days, but I was determined to see Centre Court. So at the

Two great Yugoslav Champions: Goran Ivanišević (*below, right*) and Marin Čilić (*below*).

Centre Court - South West Hall

end of one of the days, a group of us from the German team sneaked into one of the last matches in the evening. As I walked in, I remember thinking how beautiful it was, almost like walking into a church. I was really quiet and in awe of the place. This was the arena that had hosted so many great matches, many of which I'd seen on television, and I was finally there. I was almost lost for words. In real life it looked a little smaller than it does on TV – the camera angles make it look bigger, but it's more intimate in real life.

As I left Wimbledon and London, I felt I'd achieved something. I'd played on grass, I'd played at Wimbledon and I'd been into Centre Court. If I never had the chance to play there ever again, at least I had done it once.

***Left:* Walking on to Centre Court is almost like walking into a church. You're in awe of the place.**

Chapter 2

Deciding to be a professional (1983–84)

'My son is not for sale.'

As someone who won Wimbledon three times – along with three other majors, two Davis Cups and an Olympic gold medal – it may be hard to believe that it was a real act of faith for my parents to allow me to even aspire to be a professional tennis player. There was a seven-month battle between my parents and me that started in November 1983 and just about finished in June 1984, and even then it took another year for the battle to be completely won. Obviously Wimbledon played a part in convincing my family, but Wimbledon very nearly lost me the battle too.

In my family, sport wasn't a job. My father was an architect, his children were well educated, so the idea was that we would go to university or some course of study and get a proper job. Sport was for fun and good health, but not a serious profession. The problem for my parents was that they had a son who was good at sports, and they weren't quite sure what to do about it. So they supported me but didn't take my tennis too seriously, hoping I wouldn't succeed. Yet the more they hoped for that, the more I succeeded.

By 15, I was the hottest potential property in the tennis world, so the likes of Mark McCormack (the founder and head of the International Management Group, the first large-scale player management agency) and Donald Dell (the head of IMG's rival ProServ) both came to Leimen. McCormack turned up first, bringing an interpreter, and spoke to my father about signing me. But he made a big mistake – he asked my father how much money he wanted for my signature. My father bristled and

ellesse
ellesse
ellesse

Above: **My first ever tournament on grass at the Thames Ditton Club in June 1982. I think I'm the boy in the white top and blue tracksuit trousers lounging on the grassy bank, just to the left of the player diving for the volley. I liked his style...**

replied, 'My son is not for sale, here is the door Mr McCormack.' And something similar happened with Dell a few days later.

I later learned that at the 1983 French Open junior championship, when I was playing the Australian Mark Kratzmann in the semi-finals, McCormack sat watching the match with Ion Ţiriac, discussing who would sign whom. The story goes that they made a bet that whoever won the semi-final would get signed by McCormack and Ţiriac would sign whoever lost. McCormack obviously believed my father would relent, but he never got the chance to try, because Kratzmann beat me in three sets.

So Ţiriac then turned up in Leimen. Legend has it he drove up in a Rolls-Royce – he didn't, he came in his Mercedes, because he wasn't looking to impress with his money. Instead he did something very smart. He befriended my mother, and particularly admired her cooking – she's known in the family as a good cook and like all German housewives was very keen for her guests to feel well fed with well cooked food. So Ţiriac ate a lot and complimented her on her cooking, and thereby opened

Right: **The match between Mark Kratzmann and me at the French Open Junior Championship in 1983 had a bearing on my career in more ways than one.**

BASF

Above: **Ion Ţiriac persuaded my parents to allow me to attempt to become a professional tennis player. We've remained close over the years.**

the door through my mother to a long discussion with both her and my father.

His pitch was very different from McCormack's and Dell's. For a start he spoke German, which was a big advantage, and he was friends with Günther Bosch, the national coach of Germany who, like Ţiriac, was born in Romania and who my parents knew a little. But Ţiriac's strongest argument was that he had a son, Alexandre (known as 'Ion Ion'), who was a bit younger than me, and he said he would watch over me the way he would watch over his son – in other words he'd take on the family role. He was effectively saying, 'This is a business, but I'm a father too, and I'm a European.' I think my parents, especially my mother, felt more reassured by that approach.

So at 15, Ţiriac became my manager, and around my 16th birthday he confronted me with the proposition: 'well Boris, you're 16, if you want to be a professional tennis player you have to quit school'. He may have gained sufficient trust from my parents to get my signature, but I knew that convincing my mother and father, and even my sister, that I should leave school to become a professional sportsman at 16 was a no-no.

Some aspects of my education have got lost in translation over the years. There's been a general view that, educationally, I came from the woods and didn't know how to read and write. I was actually at a 'Gymnasium', the German word for grammar school in a selective system where the academically brightest kids go to the grammar school while those with more practical interests go to technical schools called 'Realschule' and 'Hauptschule'. And my school was a tough one academically from which lots of kids went on to university. So I was fully expected to leave school at 19 with my 'Abitur', the German equivalent of A-Levels or baccalaureate, and to my parents the idea of my leaving school at 16 to do sport was almost unthinkable.

So, we had this big discussion, which went on for six or seven months. I didn't need to be convinced, but I thought it would be a miracle if Ţiriac could persuade my family. I thought it would never happen, but after six months they negotiated a two-year leave of absence for me from school. I don't know what Ţiriac did, what charms he used, but he did it. I had to speak to the principal of my school, Erich Fritsch of the Helmholtz Gymnasium in Heidelberg, and explain why I really wanted to do this. Herr Fritsch spoke to my subconscious: he said, 'Boris be careful, if something happens to your knee or ankle, where are you then?' He had a point, but I wanted to do it, so we agreed that he would hold my education open for two years.

So, I had my clearance to become a tennis professional without endangering my education. It was only a two-year window of opportunity, but at 16, two years seems like a lifetime. I headed to my first tournament as a professional: the Wimbledon qualifying event.

I've played on many tennis courts in my life, and the ones used for the Wimbledon qualifying event were probably the worst I've ever encountered. For players ranked between about 110 and 250, there's a chance to get into Wimbledon through what we call 'qualies'. This is a tournament with 128 players, and not one winner but 16. If you win three rounds, you end up as one of the 16 players who get into the main Wimbledon draw. For a 16-year-old just given clearance to see if he could make it as a tennis pro, having a chance to play the Wimbledon qualies was something close to nirvana, although the spirits sank when I started playing on the courts.

The Wimbledon qualies take place in Roehampton, a suburb of London a few miles from Wimbledon. Normally it's a park, almost a common, but the week before the tournament they paint white lines and say it's now a tennis court, on which one of the most prestigious qualifying tournaments in the world gets played. The bounces were up and down, left and right, or no bounce to speak of – it was dreadful. But that's when you really learn how to take the ball early, how to volley, and not lose your serve, or your mind. There were 10 courts in a row so balls come onto your court, or you hit balls on other courts. It can be very confusing.

But I found a way. The first opponent I beat was an Australian called Greg Whitecross, then a Japanese player by the name of Shozo Shiraishi. Both were in two straight sets and that took me into my first ever match played over the best of five sets. The last round of qualifying is best-of-five, and I remember talking to Peter Pfannkuch, the coach responsible for the German juniors, telling him I was so afraid that I wouldn't last four or five sets because I'd never played that long. He just laughed and said, 'Boris you'll beat him in three anyway.' I was still worried whether I'd be fit enough if I lost the first set, but he laughed it off. And he was right – I won in straight sets against an American, Bruce Kleege.

Having qualified for the Wimbledon main draw, I really felt I'd arrived. It felt very different walking through the gates compared to the previous year. There was a sense of belonging, a sense that I'd earned it, satisfaction that I hadn't needed a wildcard. And there was also a change of hotel. For the qualifying we stayed in a Bed & Breakfast, while the main draw players stay for free in the Gloucester Hotel in Kensington, which in 1984 I thought was the best hotel in the world. That was quite a trip. Qualifying finished on Thursday or Friday, we then changed hotels, and as I came down for breakfast on Saturday, I felt like the king of the castle as I mingled with the main draw players.

The draw came out, and I was to face Blaine Willenborg. He was a very good American college player, but I knew very little about him. So I asked around and was told he had a big forehand and a big serve, but he was a shortish guy who apparently preferred clay. It was the second day of the tournament, and as we walked out to play on one of the courts between Centre and No. 1 Court, somewhere between 14 and 17, I thought 'This is it, you're playing in the main draw at Wimbledon now'. I was excited but also nervous.

Just over an hour later, with the score at 6-0, 6-0, 2-0, I finally felt I was in control. Yes, I won 14 games in a row in my very first match at Wimbledon. The weirdest thing is that it felt very normal – I felt totally at ease, I was seeing the ball like a pumpkin; I couldn't miss a thing. I began to think I could be in the second round in 20 minutes, and that was when he got into the match. He won his first game and ended up winning three more, but I held on to the break of serve and served it out at 5-4.

So I'd won my first match at Wimbledon, but I wasn't going to win my second. I was up against Nduka Odizor, a grass court specialist from Nigeria. He'd developed his tennis in America and was a good serve-volley player, which was the way to play on grass in those days. He was clearly the favourite, so people told me to do my best and not to be too upset if I lost. We played on the old Court 13 at the southern end of the ground (now the site for the current No. 2 Court), and with me leading 6-3, 6-4, 4-2 he retired. I don't know how injured he really was – he's a proud African, he was playing against a 16-year-old who he was supposed to beat; I think if he was really injured he'd have retired in the first set. I like the guy and I don't want to read too much into it, but I think there must have been some embarrassment at play, and when I broke him to lead 4-2 in the third set I suspect that made his arm feel worse, and he quit.

When I won my first match, people seemed to be happy for me when I came back to the locker room. After all, I was by far the youngest player there. When I won my second, I felt people were looking at me differently. The looks were saying, 'You haven't dropped a set yet, you haven't played here before – who are you, what are you doing? You're not supposed to do this.' And I was just smiling my way through. My English wasn't very good then, so I hung out with my German buddies, but I felt on a high already. This was powerful, it was giving me so much confidence, a sense of belonging – I remember thinking 'this is what I'm good at'.

Above: **The courts used for Wimbledon 'qualies' were the worst I'd ever played on. Based at the Bank of England Sports Centre in Roehampton, today they're in much better condition.**

THE CHAMPIONSHIPS WIMBLEDON
ORDER OF PLAY
TUESDAY 23rd JUNE
COURT
CENTRE
No.1
No.2
No.3
No.4
No.5
No.6
No.7
No.8
No.9
No.10
No.11
No.12
MATCH 1
MATCH 2
MATCH 3
MATCH 4
MATCH 5
Venus WILLIAMS v Stefanie VOEGELE
Juan Martin DEL POTRO v Arnaud CLEMENT
Caroline WOZNIACKI v Kimiko DATE KRUMM
Julia GOERGES v Jelena JANKOVIC
Nikolay DAVYDENKO v Daniel EVANS
Victor HANESCU v Ivan NAVARRO
Galina VOSKOBOEVA v Na LI
Jelena DOKIC v Tatjana MALEK
Olga GOVORTSOVA v Tatiana PEREBIYNIS
Anastasija SEVASTOVA v Kateryna BONDARENKO
Oscar HERNANDEZ v Leonardo MAYER
Bethanie MATTEK-SANDS
Iveta BENESOVA
Maria KIRILENKO
Bjorn PHAU
Teimuraz GABASHVILI
Nicolas LAPENTTI
Jeremy CHARDY v Andy RODDICK
Dinara SAFINA v Lourdes DOMINGUEZ LINO
Michael LLODRA v Joshua GOODALL
Tommy HAAS v Alexander PEYA
Patricia MAYR v Anne KEOTHAVONG
Marta DOMACHOWSKA v Anabel MEDINA GARRIGUES
Grigor DIMITROV v Igor KUNITSYN
Fabio FOGNINI v Denis ISTOMIN
Monica NICULESCU v Yaroslava SHVEDOVA
Benjamin BECKER v Roko KARANUSIC
Nicole VAIDISOVA v Rossana DE LOS RIOS
Kevin KIM
Sybille BAMMER
Alberta BRIANTI
Andy MURRAY v Robert KENDRICK
Juan Carlos FERRERO v Mikhail YOUZHNY
Alex BOGDANOVIC v Tomas BERDYCH
Lleyton HEWITT v Robby GINEPRI
Radek STEPANEK v Alejandro FALLA
Taylor DENT v Daniel GIMENO-TRAVER
Riccardo GHEDIN v Ernests GULBIS
Nuria LLAGOSTERA VIVES v Flavia PENNETTA
Brian DABUL v Viktor TROICKI
Thiago ALVES v Andrei PAVEL
Christophe ROCHUS v Pablo CUEVAS
Stanislas WAWRINKA v Eduardo SCHWANK
Wayne ODESNIK
Stephanie DUBOIS
Philipp PETZSCHNER
Sabine LISICKI
Dmitry TURSUNOV
Bobby REYNOLDS v Gilles SIMON
Fabrice SANTORO v Nicolas KIEFER
Lucie HRADECKA v Ana IVANOVIC
Kristina KUCOVA v Aiko NAKAMURA
Alexa GLATCH v Shuai PENG
Pauline PARMENTIER v Akgul AMANMURADOVA
Vania KING v Mariya KORYTTSEVA
Kirsten FLIPKENS v Agnes SZAVAY
Potito STARACE v Jose ACASUSO
Pablo ANDUJAR
Ekaterina MAKAROVA
Jesse LEVINE v Marat SAFIN
Akiko MORIGAMI v Svetlana KUZNETSOVA
Amelie MAURESMO v Melinda CZINK

Left and above: **128 players enter the draw for Wimbledon, which takes place just before the Championship commences at the end of June. By the middle weekend only 24 singles players remain in the draw and the atmosphere in the locker room completely changes.**

My third round match was on the Saturday, and by the middle weekend the place changes in character. The locker room becomes less crowded, simply because there are fewer people around – you start with 128 players in the singles draw, and by the weekend you're down to 24. But it also becomes a much colder place, emotionally. People watch you a lot more. At first they were happy for me, but by the time I'd beaten Odizor they were less friendly; they didn't interact so much and were less chatty – I felt an antipathy that reflected the fact that I was a threat.

My match was being billed as a Saturday afternoon blockbuster. I was up against Bill Scanlon, one of the best grass court players in the world, and on the old Court 2, which was known as 'the graveyard' because of all the big names who had lost there over the years. Scanlon was ranked 17 when I played him and had won a 'golden set' the previous year (6-0, without losing a point); he was also the player who John McEnroe wasn't looking forward to playing in the round of 16. In fact Scanlon was someone nobody liked to play on grass – he had a good game, and a very strong personality (he works in personal financial investment now). But by then people were saying 'who's this young kid from West Germany?' German television had picked it up, it was Saturday afternoon, and it was the match of the day, because the winner would play McEnroe in the fourth round and McEnroe hadn't lost at Wimbledon for three years. So the hype was already promoting either a 'McEnroe-Scanlon' match or a possible 'McEnroe-Becker' match on the Monday. I became aware that I was involved in a real spectacle.

I played well. I lost the first set but I won the second. The third was tight – I lost it on the tiebreak, but I then got an early break in the fourth and was really enjoying it. I knew this guy was really good, but I was sticking with him and he wasn't killing me. I was really revelling in the moment.

But I was beginning to get tired. I wasn't used to best-of-five sets matches. I was still confident, but I was running on empty, which perhaps made me quite dangerous because I had nothing to lose. Then at 2-1 in the fourth set I served, I came to the net, I did my 'split step', which is how you stop your forward run in readiness for the volley, and my ankle gave way. I twisted it badly – it was a really bad sprain. I hobbled to the net but I couldn't even walk off court. The physio, Bill Norris, came and talked to me. He rattled away in English, and I didn't understand a word he said. It was a big drama – they carried me off on a stretcher, my ankle swelling up like a golf ball. I went for an MRI scan as quickly as I could, and it revealed that, of the three ligaments in the ankle, two were torn.

Clearly the story was that this young German player had been carried off on a stretcher with a horrible injury, and I later learned that some people wondered whether it might end my career. But I didn't mind, I was at peace. I'd played for two hours with Bill Scanlon, feeling the ball really well. I felt the

Right: **Here I am in action at the German Youth Championships in 1984.**

ankle would heal, and when it did, I'd gained so much confidence from the two wins and giving Scanlon a real run for his money, that I could be optimistic about the future.

While I was at peace, my mother reacted very differently. She was actually relieved that I'd torn the ligaments. That sounds strange, but you have to go back to the big argument in my family that sport wasn't a proper job. Ţiriac had somehow persuaded my parents that my prospects of making it as a professional were sufficiently good that I should put my education on hold for two years, but they were still worried that an injury might kill my tennis career stone dead. So here, in my very first tournament as a professional on my leave of absence, I play the Wimbledon qualies, I make it to the main draw, and then I tear ligaments in my ankle on the Saturday, just as my parents and the principal of my school had feared. On Sunday I flew home, on Monday I had surgery in Heidelberg. And as I was convalescing, my mother said to me, 'I told you so, I told you so. Now you'd better get your rehab, and then I think it's time for you to go back to school.'

***Left:* It was when I did my 'split step' in the fourth set against Bill Scanlon that I tore my ankle ligaments in my first appearance at Wimbledon in 1984. I was disappointed but encouraged by my debut at the All England Club.**

1985

So what else was going on in the world in 1985 when I won Wimbledon?

I remember Live Aid very well, a massive concert in Wembley Stadium organised by Bob Geldof. These days he's a good friend of mine, but we didn't know each other then – Live Aid was only a week after I'd won Wimbledon. I watched on television, and remember being very moved by it.

After Wimbledon, I signed a contract to become an ambassador for Coca-Cola. It was mainly to promote New Coke, as the company had changed the formula and was marketing the original drink as Coke Classic. Coke Classic massively outsold New Coke, and New Coke was abandoned after three months, but my contract was for five years so I spent most of it promoting the original drink.

I remember the Heysel Stadium disaster in which 39 football fans were killed at the European Cup final. That kind of event sends a little shiver through me, because it shows what can happen in a big sporting event. Tennis players are very close to the fans, some of whom can be a bit crazy, especially in Davis Cup matches, so you're alert to things like that. We're also alert to air disasters because we use planes so much, and there were a lot of plane crashes that year.

Although I don't remember it, the first smoking ban in restaurants in America came into effect in Aspen, Colorado. I completely agree with being very sensitive about smoking and tobacco, but it shouldn't be a prison term if you do smoke. We are restricting our freedom more and more every year, and I don't think that's right. These days I smoke cigars; I don't want restaurants to be full of smoke, but I do feel there should be a place for people who want to smoke to do so, maybe at a designated bar.

It's amazing to think that Microsoft released the first version of Windows, Windows 1.0, in 1985. The news of that passed me by, because I wasn't into computers until much later, but from little beginnings came something that has changed the world.

The first mobile phone call was also made that year.

The Tommy Hilfiger brand was established in 1985. I know Tommy and his wife very well these days, he's a great tennis fan. In fact Tommy, like me, is an adviser to the ATP, albeit on a different advisory board than mine.

And I won Wimbledon playing in very short shorts (we all did in those days) and with the last-ever shot with a white tennis ball! Actually, that's not strictly true, they played the mixed doubles final after the men's singles, but it was the last day white balls were used at Wimbledon. The All England Club finally acceded to television's request for a more visible yellow ball the following year.

Below: **Bob Geldof talks to the audience at Live Aid in 1985. He's a good friend of mine today.**

Chapter 3

Winning Wimbledon at 17 (1985)

'You're on some unbelievable ride.'

'Now hold on, Mum,' I said. 'Let me have my rehab, and then I can at least play the year through, so I only lose one year of my education.' This was the conversation after I came out of ankle surgery in Heidelberg, a couple of days after being carried off on a stretcher from my match with Bill Scanlon at Wimbledon. It was just a few weeks earlier that Ţiriac and I had persuaded them to put my education on hold for two years, yet despite what I considered the great success of five wins at Wimbledon – three in qualifying, two in the main draw – and a creditable defeat, I was right back in my battle to be a tennis professional. I really had to fight off my parents' attempts at getting me to end all thoughts of a professional career there and then. They felt their words of caution had been proved right by my ankle injury, and you can understand that. But they did accept that I should at least get fit and play the year out, so my tennis career was back on.

The rehabilitation techniques weren't as good then as they are now, so it was another eight weeks before I was back in a competitive match, and my next tournament was the 1985 US Open juniors. I reached the final, and waiting for me was Mark Kratzmann, the Aussie who had beaten me in the French Open semis. He won again, more easily this time (6-3, 7-6), but this proved to be a momentous day for me.

The boys' singles final took place on Saturday morning. Although I lost, I then witnessed one of the best Saturdays ever in tennis. At that time the US Open operated what it called 'Super Saturday', a day with both men's semi-finals, and the women's singles final sandwiched in between. It was crazy scheduling for the players, but wonderful for the fans who had tickets. That particular Super Saturday started with Cash-Lendl, then there was the women's final, Evert against Navratilova, followed by McEnroe-Connors. I went straight from the boys' final ceremony to Stadium Court to watch Cash-Lendl, and I stayed there all day, still in my tennis clothes, and that changed my tennis life forever. I was so fascinated by all six players that

Above: **'Super Saturday' at the US Open in 1984 pretty much changed my life from a tennis point of view. Seeing players like McEnroe, Evert and Navratilova was an honour and one of the best days of my life.**

Above: **Guillermo Vilas was one of the biggest names in Ion Ţiriac's roster and one of my early hitting partners.**

I watched all day without even showering, still with my ankle taped from the junior final. That was the best day of my life at that point – I was hooked. Although they didn't know it at the time, my parents had lost the battle to prevent me from being a professional tennis player.

And yet, few people realise that I went through a real crisis of confidence about six months before I won Wimbledon. I was ready to quit. So you could say the story of my Wimbledon triumph began in South Africa in November 1984.

After the US Open, I'd been enthusiastic about my practice, which even involved getting up at five in the morning when we were in Basel. One of the biggest names in Ţiriac's stable of players was Guillermo Vilas, and he had this habit of practising from six to eight in the morning when everything was quiet. So we had to be at the stadium by six, and after our practice he'd send me running all the way up the stairs of the enormous St Jakobs-Halle where the Basel tournament is played. You had to be fit to make it to the top of that place, especially after two hours hitting with Vilas.

My results were OK, but not as good as I wanted them to be. I lost to Jakob Hlasek in Basel, I won a round in Vienna and the tournament in London's Wembley Arena, but lost second round at both. Two weeks later I was in South Africa for the SA Open at Ellis Park, Johannesburg, and it was hot. The Ţiriac squad was all together – Vilas, Leconte, Živojinović, Năstase, and me – it was a great team. I played the qualifying tournament, I won the first two rounds, but in the final qualifying round I got heatstroke and I had to retire. I was in tears afterwards. I had a long discussion with Ţiriac, and I had a sort of breakdown. I said 'Ion, I don't think I can do this. This is too hard. I don't think I can make it as a player. I'm practising all these hours, and I can hardly win a match – this is impossible. A few months ago I was in the third round at Wimbledon, and now I'm losing to all these guys, I can't get through the qualifying tournaments, I'm getting heatstroke, I miss my home. I'm happy to do all this if I win, but I have no benefits when I don't win.' It was the week before my 17th birthday, and I was ranked about 110, which isn't bad for 17 but wasn't what I'd been expecting after reaching the third round at Wimbledon.

Ţiriac said to me, 'Listen son, I promise you, I'll put this on paper if you want: if you continue this way of practising, I can guarantee you'll be well inside the top 50 in six months. You practise like an animal, I've never seen anyone work like you do – you put it all out there, you bleed, and you're willing to travel to South Africa. I understand your frustration, I understand that emotionally you're very weak now, but please hang in there.'

The following week we went to Melbourne for the Australian Open, which in those days was played in early December. And I got to the quarter-finals. Beating Rick Meyer in the first round was important, but it was the win over Tim Mayotte in the second round that was the breakthrough. It was the first time since Wimbledon that I'd won two consecutive matches in a men's event, and I was on cloud nine – a week after wanting to quit! Mayotte is one of the best-ever players on grass, so

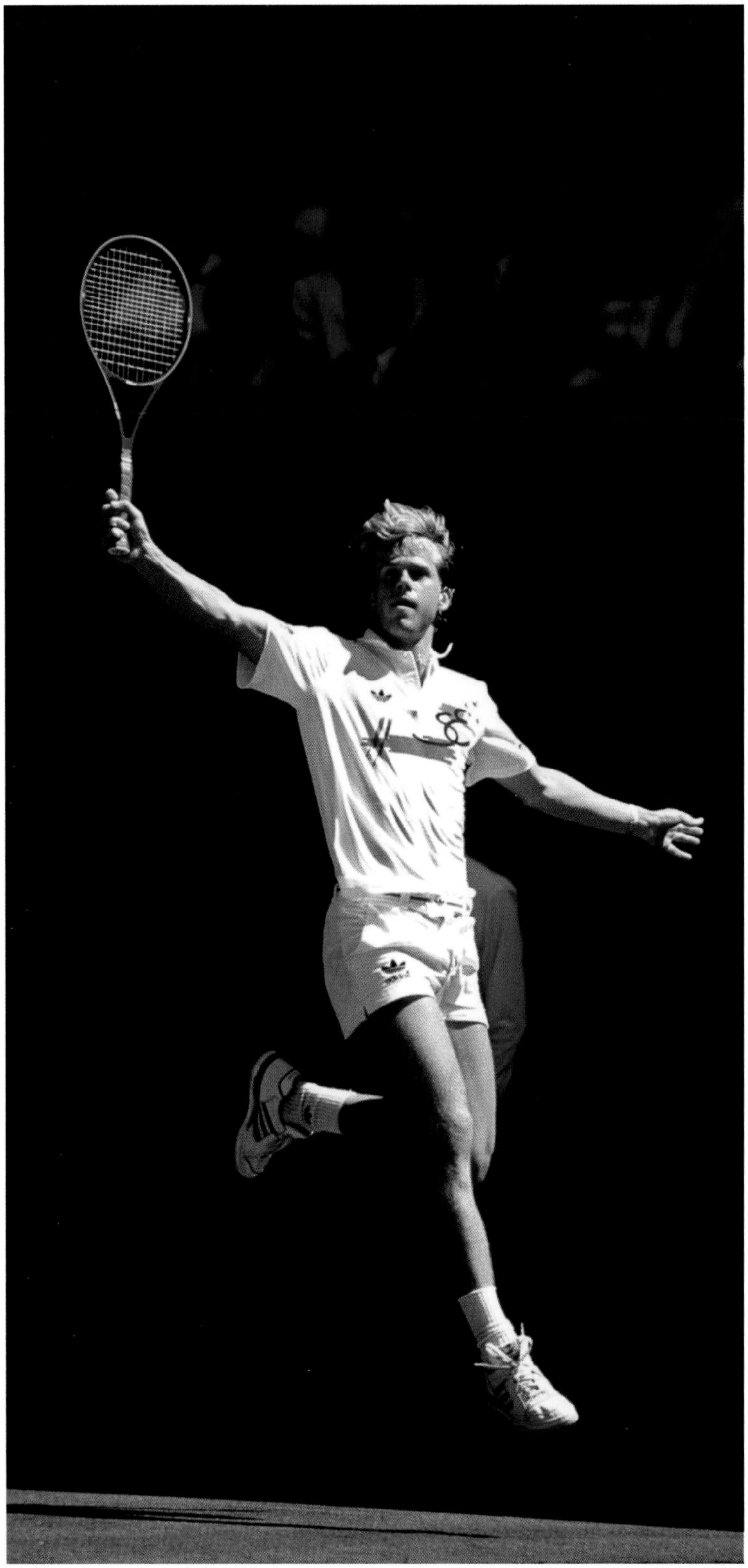

beating him in four sets was the turning point. I lost to Ben Testerman in the quarters, but I felt good and I was up to 55 in the rankings after the Australian Open. So what Ţiriac promised me I'd achieve in six months I'd almost achieved two weeks later. I was so relieved when I went home for Christmas. My mother, bless her, greeted me with 'Oh God, son, what are you doing – playing so well?'

My run at the Australian Open meant I'd get into the main draw of all the tournaments I wanted to play, but in early February there was a special tournament called the Young Masters, which took place in Birmingham. This was for the best players in the world under 21, so both juniors and the best of the young touring professionals. It's an idea that could be revived today, as today's 18–21-year-olds seem to have greater trouble establishing themselves on the main tour than the teenagers in the 1980s. And who do I play in the final but Stefan Edberg? It was my first match that went to five sets, and I beat him. Everyone expected him to win – he'd won all four junior Slams in 1983, he had this beautiful fluent style, and I'd never beaten him until then. So getting to the quarters in Australia and then beating Edberg for the first time in my first five-setter – that was my big exclamation mark, my statement to the world. And winning that five-setter was very important when I had to play two five-setters at Wimbledon five months later.

***Left:* I beat Stefan Edberg in the final of the Young Masters in Birmingham in my first ever five-setter.**

The day after Birmingham I flew to Portland, Oregon, to play an exhibition tournament. I wasn't very good at exhibitions, because I always took every match so seriously. This was an exhibition where you had to play four matches to win the tournament, and I did – I think I beat Jimmy Connors in the final. So I'd won two tournaments in successive weeks against decent players. On the plane from Portland to my next tournament in Philadelphia, I was laughing and joking at the back of the plane with some other players when Ţiriac came and spoke to me. 'Son,' he said, 'you better get ready because you're on some unbelievable ride. This is real, this isn't just a lucky run; this is proper world-class tennis you're playing. If you stay healthy, I don't know who can stop you.'

When you look back on my results, I was very consistent. I wasn't winning everything, but the thing with most 17-year-olds is that they have some good results without being able to sustain it. I was playing well week-by-week. I was happy again, I loved the tennis, and the travelling, and the hotels – I couldn't get enough. I left home in early January, played singles and doubles every week, and didn't go home until April – for Davis Cup when we beat Spain in two days in my first Davis Cup tie. That was the first time they really took notice of me in Germany; they didn't follow tennis much in those days, at least not when you play in Philadelphia or Memphis.

I then played the clay court season, winning a few rounds, including beating Ilie Năstase in Monte Carlo. Ţiriac had warned me about Năstase and told me he would try and get in my head, and he did – I was 0-3 down in quick time, with Ţiriac screaming 'Concentrate, focus' from the stands. Well I did and ended up beating Năstase 6-4, 6-1. I then won four rounds in Rome and reached the semi-finals.

I was now six weeks short of my Wimbledon title, and when you look back there were small signs that the world was taking notice of me. In the first round of the French Open, I played

Above: **I hold the trophy after beating Johan Kriek in the 1985 Queen's final. He shocked the press by saying I could win Wimbledon.**

Vitas Gerulaitis – a fading top player against a 17-year-old German – yet they put the match on the Centre Court. I beat him in four sets, before losing to Mats Wilander in the second round. That was no embarrassment, and it also meant I had time to prepare for the grass court season.

As Ţiriac was never a fan of too much down time, he suggested I play the tournament on the grass of Beckenham in south London, which took place in the second week of the French Open. This was another tournament where the courts are not regular grass courts. They're marked out on a cricket field, and they're pretty terrible, but it's great practice. I reached the semi-finals, where I lost to Mayotte in three sets, so it was a good week. That was the Saturday, the much bigger tournament at London's Queen's Club started on the Monday, and I was just in the flow of things. No injuries, confident, young, back on grass, my ankle fully healed, and I was playing every week.

I wasn't seeded for Queen's but I went through the rounds, and on the Friday I played two matches because of rain – I played my third round in the morning and quarter-final in the afternoon. But it didn't matter, I was like a bull, I could have played 10 sets that day. I beat David Pate in the morning, and Pat Cash in the afternoon – 6-4, 6-4.

By then there was the sense that something strange was going on. People were in awe, they made funny comments, such as: 'what is this, it isn't right that this guy should be winning like this.' I felt I had so much power I could hit harder than anyone else. In practice I would show off and hit even harder than I'm supposed to hit, and play with the idea that I had this power. That's where the nickname 'Boom Boom' came from. I was playing doubles with Vijay Amritraj in the spring of 1985 in Rotterdam; we got to the semi-finals and became friends, and he was the first one to nickname me 'Boom Boom' because I hit the ball so hard. Sometimes I hit it too hard when it wasn't always necessary, but that's the way I played – I had no soft

Above: **I was like a bull, I could have played 10 sets that day**

shot, which is something of a weakness, but it meant I just belted the ball.

The first inkling that I might be a contender at Wimbledon came after the Queen's final. I played Johan Kriek, who had won the Australian Open twice on grass, and I destroyed him 6-2, 6-3. In his press conference afterwards, he said, 'Listen guys, I will put money on this guy. If he serves next week the way he served this week, he will win Wimbledon.' Everybody laughed and said it was impossible. But Johan insisted: 'I've played against everyone, and I've never seen anyone with such raw power. He's confident, he's young, he doesn't think about it, he doesn't know what it means – you watch.' Everyone laughed, and made out that because Kriek had lost to a 17-year-old he just wanted to make it look better for himself. I was asked about it in my press conference but my English was very poor, and I wasn't interested in getting into a public discussion about my chances.

I must come back to the reality of the times here. Today's youngsters probably can't imagine a life without the internet – without social media, without mobile phones or smartphones. Even those of us who knew those times struggle to remember what it was like. But it was crucial to my success.

Two things were different. There was lots of anticipation building up with people starting to talk about me as a possible Wimbledon champion, but there wasn't the idea that I was the *next big thing*. I was 17, I was playing well, and tennis fans were interested, but there weren't millions of people talking me up the way there would be today. And there's no way you could keep the lid on all the anticipation today. I remember that, as a 17-year-old who just six months earlier was struggling with motivation and belief, who'd just won Queen's, it was a hell of a challenge to keep it all in perspective. But I didn't know what it meant to the world – I was in a complete bubble, I was just thinking day-to-day. Ţiriac was very smart about not allowing me to break out – to return to Leimen or Heidelberg or wherever. I was almost a tennis machine. I was driven – I loved it, otherwise I wouldn't have done it – but I wasn't allowed any breaks at all. I was inside a bubble the whole time, and that saved me.

Another thing happened that, again, you just couldn't keep quiet now. My grandfather Franz, after whom I have my middle name, died on the Friday before Wimbledon started. I loved him very much and was sad to miss his funeral, but my mother felt it was best for me not to know that he had left us, and to give me the information after the tournament, as it would have affected me. So she kept it quiet for more than two weeks – that's unthinkable today.

Because I liked the Gloucester Hotel so much in 1984, I wanted to stay there for Queen's, so I did. I won the tournament, and superstition means you never want to change hotel and I stayed in the Gloucester for the duration of the Wimbledon Championships too. I practised with many of the top players the week between the two tournaments,

***Left:* Winning that day was a great feeling.**

not McEnroe or Connors but against Anders Järryd, Joakim Nyström and Mats Wilander, and my fellow countrymen Andreas Maurer and Michael Westphal. I hadn't played any of the big names in a big match, except Wilander at the French Open. I remember the adulation and the admiration, it obviously felt very good and it made me smile, I was proud of what I'd achieved, and I felt almost invincible, and I loved it a lot. But I didn't feel cocky. Nowadays people talk about the pressure to do it again, to defend what you had, but I remember thinking the pressure had gone because I'd done it. I'd won Queen's so the pressure was off. I had nothing to prove.

I wasn't seeded at Wimbledon. In those days there were only 16 seeds and I was 20th in the rankings with not enough of a record on grass to impress the seeding committee, so I was still somewhat under the radar. And any idea of winning Wimbledon was almost blown away in the first round.

Throughout much of my childhood I had had a goal to one day play on Centre Court, and I achieved it on day one. Even though I wasn't seeded and drew the world No. 62 Hank Pfister in my first match, they put me on Centre on the opening day. Think about it: an unseeded West German against an unseeded American, third match on the first day on Centre Court! That was pretty gutsy. In those days there was no roof and they started at 2pm, so it was getting dark when we came on court. I was nervous when I walked out; I was overexcited and I didn't know about the footing because it was very slippery – my footing was always the strong part of my game but I was sliding a lot, probably more because of nervousness and insecurities than the first-day slipperiness of the court. I also had to bow to the Royal Box. I felt like I was watching a movie – I was outside my body watching me play on Centre Court at Wimbledon.

Perhaps because of not being in the moment, I dropped my serve early, and that was enough to lose the first set 6-4. That woke me up. Early in the second I began to focus on the match, and from then I was OK. Due to the late start, I wasn't going to win on that first day after dropping the first set, so the match was postponed. But as I left the court, I was so happy because I'd played on Centre Court. I remember Ţiriac driving me home that night, and I said 'See Ion, I've played on Centre Court, and now I can play on Centre Court two days running!'

Not a lot of people know this, but I only once lost an interrupted match at Wimbledon. That was the 1988 final – other than that, I was unbeatable if there was an overnight interruption, whether for a rain delay or due to fading light. I felt comfortable, I got to know the opponent, I got to know the place, so the longer it went on the more comfortable I became. And I beat Pfister fairly easily on the Tuesday.

Then on Wednesday I played Matt Anger on No. 2 Court. I thought 'I'm in the tournament, this is great' but Anger had a good game on grass. I beat him 6-0, 6-1, 6-3. On grass that shouldn't happen – you don't beat players like that. You can beat them 6-4, 6-3, 7-6, that's OK, but not 6-0, 6-1, 6-3. People started asking 'Who is this guy, what's he doing?' The looks I got, even if I saw most of them via the mirrors in the locker room, seemed to say 'What are you doing?' and 'You're not supposed to be doing this!'

Yet I was comfortable, totally at ease in that environment and felt I belonged there. People told me later that I walked through the locker room as if I owned the place already, the way I walked around with my shoulders back. I didn't do it on purpose, but when I'm comfortable this is probably how I act, this is who I am. It's not an act I put on; I've always been like that, I've never been timid or in awe of a situation. I was like that in my school class, I was very confident about myself early on – I had a couple of girlfriends early that I wasn't supposed to have, but because of my confidence and my way of being they couldn't help themselves. It had nothing to do with tennis.

***Right:* I always felt confident on a tennis court, and I think that's something that frightened them.**

BASF

Or I'd go out on a Saturday night in Heidelberg at 15 or 16, and my mother, father and sister were confident that I wouldn't get into trouble and I'd be home at 12 or one o'clock on the last train. My upbringing was like that; they instilled a lot of confidence in me that I would know what's right. So the attitude people were picking up in the locker room was this sense of belonging and confidence – not arrogance. I was shy when I spoke, but very confident in my actions. I always felt confident on a tennis court, and I think that's something that frightened them. It looked so natural, it wasn't staged or a persona that I had to put on, it was just me being myself.

The media interest started to pick up after the Anger match, but I didn't do many extra interviews – Ţiriac and Bosch were very careful to keep me in the bubble. It soon took off after the third round match. Although my English wasn't good, I wasn't afraid of the stage, I'm very comfortable performing, so I was happy to do the interviews that Ţiriac said were OK. Despite my English, I still felt I had something to say. A drive of wanting to communicate something was very much there.

My third match was pure drama. It was on No. 2 Court against Joakim Nyström, a guy who was a regular in the top 10 at the time. I didn't know what to expect but he had one of the best returns in the game, and his way of playing was very well suited to beating me. My serving and volleying, and chipping and charging, played totally into his strengths, and I was told it would be tough. In hindsight he should have beaten me: he served for the match twice in a row in the fifth set, and he could have easily won, but he didn't. When people ask me how I came through what was only my second five-set match, and against a top player in the third round at Wimbledon, I often tell them that sometimes you have to be prepared to lose in order to win. You have to take the chance, and say 'this might go wrong but I have to do it'. I was playing aggressively, approaching the net, hitting the ball hard on my return, accepting that this could go into the net, but I still had to do it. And I think that threw him off. I wasn't trying to be careful all of a sudden and just hope – I was going for my shots, and I kept on coming. It was as if he thought, 'What do I have to do? – I've broken him twice, I've passed him 10 times, I've lobbed him, and he still comes in to my backhand! Is he crazy?' But that was the only way I could play. It's easier said than done, but you have to go for your shots. I won 9-7 in the fifth.

That was Saturday afternoon. The following day was the middle Sunday rest day, and the media interest picked up. I started to talk a bit more than I should have. You know how it is – people come and talk, and you're proud of your achievement, so you chat a little bit, but every chat takes away a bit of your energy and concentration. Practice on that Sunday was hard; I felt heavy after a long match and I started hurting a little. I knew I had Mayotte on Monday, a seriously good player on grass. We had a bit of a track record – I'd beaten him on grass at Melbourne six months earlier, and he'd beaten me on grass at Beckenham.

To most people, the win against Nyström should have been the end of the line. This 17-year-old wins Queen's, wins a dramatic five-setter against the world No. 8 to reach the second week, but you can only go so far. And when I lost the third set, which meant I'd have to go five sets again, everything pointed to my going out of the tournament. Physically I was fine, but mentally I was starting to tire a little. I got frustrated and angry, I screamed, I may even have broken a racket – I was just showing frustration and the first signs of weaknesses.

We played on Court 14 where the crowd is very close to the action, and that probably saved me. He won the third set on the tiebreak, and at that point I really felt tired and wounded. And then something amazing happened.

***Left:* I play a volley at Wimbledon in June 1985.**

B BECKER

Remember the previous year against Bill Scanlon? – I'd just lost the third set on the tiebreak, but I'd broken early in the fourth when my ankle went. Well I broke Mayotte early in the fourth, so I'm leading 2-1 and serving. And what happens? – I twist the exact same ankle as I twisted a year before on the exact same move. I served, came into the net, and turned the ankle doing my split step. I was on the floor in pain, I was frustrated, and at that moment I'd had enough. I looked up to Ţiriac and Bosch and signalled with my hands that it was over – that I wanted to shake hands and get out of there.

We then enter a scarcely credible dream sequence. Fortunately for me, Mayotte is too far away from the net. If he'd have been at the net I would have shaken hands for sure, but he's at the baseline. I look at the umpire, and spread my hands in the gesture that means it's over, but the umpire is a little slow to be certain what I'm saying. The next thing I hear is Ţiriac at the side of the court screaming at me – in German, because if he'd done it in English I could have been penalised for being coached – 'take an injury timeout, take an injury timeout!'

I'm still in shock and frustrated so I look at him and signal 'Enough, I want to quit'.

Mayotte walks to the net.

'Take a timeout!' screams Ţiriac again. And in a split second, I process what Ion is saying. So I clarify to the umpire that what I'm signalling is that I want to take an injury timeout. Mayotte then arrives at the net – if he had got there a moment earlier the match would be over. As it is, the trainer is called. The trainer, Bill Norris who later became a good friend, takes an age to reach the court, and in the time I'm waiting, my emotions calm down. Bill checks the ankle and says nothing was broken – it's swollen but not broken. He tapes it and gives me anti-inflammatories which he warns me won't kick in for another 20 minutes.

From that point I relaxed. I thought I'd lost the match but miraculously I was still in it. I won the fourth set on the tiebreak, and then with the anti-inflammatories kicking in I was relaxed and pain-free in the fifth set. And poor old Tim felt the tension of feeling he should have won the match – he didn't know how badly injured I was, whether I was faking it, and the rest of the match was mine (I took the fifth set 6-2). He never held it against me, it was just part of the game. And I was too young for gamesmanship – I had a genuinely swollen ankle.

After that, I had the feeling I'd come back from the dead. What was there to lose now? I was in the quarter-finals and I was playing my old practice partner and friend Henri Leconte. So on my day off between the Mayotte and Leconte matches, I didn't practice, I just had the ankle massaged and iced. There was a different energy about me now – having expected to lose the last two or three matches, I suddenly felt confident.

I'd got to know Leconte as a member of the group of players Ţiriac managed. On his day, Henri was unbeatable, but if you could get into his mind, the more predictable he became and the more fragile. We were proper hitting partners in those days, we spent a lot of time together, and I knew that I was never the best in practice. I needed the match atmosphere, while Henri was the opposite – you couldn't touch him in practice, so I always felt that if I lost a practice set to him 6-4 I was in good shape. We knew each other's psyches and weaknesses, and I knew what he didn't like better than he knew what I didn't like; I had a stronger mind. His biggest weakness was that he wasn't a competitor – he was a shotmaker: he played beautiful tennis for the spectators, he played to hit that one incredible shot off the back of five bad shots, whereas I felt I could compete with anybody.

The nature of a tournament format suits the competitor more than the shotmaker, and the further in I progressed the more aware I became that we were in a different tournament

Left: **I was on the floor in pain, I was frustrated, and at that moment I'd had enough.**

emotionally. There were fewer players around, every match was on Centre or No. 1 Court, it was quieter in the locker room, everyone was more careful, there were more media obligations – it was just a much bigger deal, every match was a final from the quarters onwards. I felt this was playing to my strengths, along with the scheduling and another twist of fate.

We were scheduled second match on Centre Court after the eagerly awaited match between the defending champion John McEnroe and the big-serving South African Kevin Curren (he played under the US flag due to issues with the apartheid regime in South Africa). McEnroe was the big favourite, but Curren beat him 6-2, 6-2, 6-4, and as I took in the enormity of the result, I thought 'Hmm, so the defending champion, somebody no-one wants to play, the champion in the last two years, is out. Let me think about this.' It was the first time I thought I might win the tournament.

Yet I didn't let it affect me as I walked out to play Leconte – I had learned my lesson from the way my mind wandered against Pfister in the first round. The place was still settling down after Curren's amazing win, but for some reason that suited me. The atmosphere is often a bit flat for the start of the second match, but I preferred playing second – I was emotionally, physically and spiritually in the match. If I played the first match, I never knew whether I'd properly arrived – occasionally I was too fresh, my body and soul weren't quite there, so playing Leconte after a shock result suited me fine. I lost the second set on the tiebreak, but I started to serve really well in the third and fourth sets. When I broke him in the third set I started to get the taste of blood – that sense of not being far away from victory. I still had to concentrate on my serve but subconsciously and emotionally I could taste the victory, and I beat him in four sets.

That made me the first German semi-finalist since Wilhelm Bungert in 1967 and everyone was now waking up to the fact that I might win the title. Fortunately my semi-final opponent Anders Järryd was not John McEnroe. He was good, he was No. 1 in doubles and sixth in singles, but he was no McEnroe or Connors. I wasn't the favourite but people were saying I could win this match.

Again, the scheduling and other results helped me. Järryd and I were scheduled second after the Curren-Connors match, and after Connors had lost 6-1, 6-1, 6-2, I went out thinking 'McEnroe's out, Connors is now out, no-one's left who has won a Grand Slam singles title – this is unbelievable.' I felt the circle coming round. And perhaps as a result, I started my own match too carefully. Anders killed me in the first set, 6-2. In the second set he had lots of chances, he had a great return against my serve, and he was close to going two sets up. So I did something different – for the first time that Wimbledon I stayed back after my second serve. Nobody thought I could play from the back of the court, but I could, and that threw him off. He had a set point for a two-sets lead, but I won the tiebreak, and then I felt in control. I knew I couldn't just serve and volley, I had to mix it up and play more clever tennis and slice my backhand more. I think he was completely taken aback by that – he didn't think I had it in me. I also think the emotional pressure of a Wimbledon semi-final got to him more than me.

People have asked me over the years whether I was ever seized by the thought that this was little me, the teenager who seven months earlier had been questioning whether he would make it as a professional, in a schoolboy-daydream scenario of being in the final of Wimbledon. The answer is no. The only time it happened was in the first set of my first match against Hank Pfister, and it never came back.

After the third set the match was called off because of rain or darkness, but I felt I could handle the situation when we resumed on Saturday. The break in proceedings also helped manage the emotions of a Wimbedon final at the tender age of 17.

The fact that my semi was carried over to Saturday meant I didn't have time to think too long about the final. I played the closing set of the Järryd match on Saturday lunchtime, which was essentially my pre-final practice; this meant I didn't have time for all the interviews, and I think it backfired on Kevin that he had the whole day off to reflect on the occasion. He had time to think about his first major final but for much of that time he didn't know who he'd be playing – I think it worked in my favour.

***Above:* A schoolboy-daydream scenario of being in the final of Wimbledon.**

On the Saturday night, we went to our usual restaurant, San Lorenzo in Beauchamp Place, and I had the same meal as I had every night – T-bone steak, pasta, tomato and mozzarella, with lemon sorbet for dessert, only water to drink, and no espresso. When we got back to the Gloucester, I had my usual hot bath, and I suddenly started to daydream about the final. I was imagining holding up the trophy. It was so clear in my head. It wasn't a conscious effort to picture what I wanted to happen, it was a dream with my eyes open – I even had a crystal clear picture of match point: that I won the match with an unreturnable serve. And then I slept really well.

I had the same warm-up partner for the semis and final, Pavel Slozil. He hit with me on the Friday, Saturday and Sunday, so I didn't have to get used to a new partner. The final was at 2pm, so we hit at noon, as two hours before the match was enough for me. We hit for 35–40 minutes, it was sunny, I felt good about being there, and I think that made a difference. I was excited to be there, whereas I felt Kevin seemed intimidated. He was 27, I was 17, so I felt I'd have more Grand Slam finals, whereas it had taken him a long time to reach his first final, so there was more pressure on him. There was also a clash of styles – I never liked to play against good returners but I was fine against a big serve; Kevin had a big serve but didn't have a good return. It meant that when I was comfortable holding my serve, I could concentrate on trying to break his serve. So I wasn't afraid in the final, especially when a couple of little omens fell in my favour.

The British have this slightly cheeky view of the Germans – that at holiday resorts the Germans get up early to drape their towels over the best sun loungers in order to reserve them for that day's sunbathing. It's not really fair, but something I did that day played right into this stereotype. I wanted the first

chair, the one nearest the Royal Box, because I'd been sitting on that chair in all my Centre Court matches, so it became a matter of superstition. But Kevin had been sitting on that chair too, so who would get it? These days there's a convention at most tournaments that the lower ranked player walks out first, but not at Wimbledon; in fact before the 2014 final I told Novak Djokovic to 'get that first chair, make sure you go out there first'. So back in 1985, I sprinted ahead when we walked out onto the grass, a bit like Nadal does after the coin toss today. That was my first victory – I got the chair I'd wanted, and that felt important.

The second victory was the toss. I'd dreamt about winning the toss, because I felt if I could hold my first service game, I could go all out to attack his opening service game before he'd got his big serve working and the nerves out of his system. I won the toss, and elected to serve.

These little things may seem insignificant now, but taken together, it meant I wasn't afraid in the final whereas he started nervously. And that meant my plan worked like clockwork. I won the first service game, Curren started to double-fault, and he lost his serve probably for the first time in the week. He soon settled down, but that break was enough for me to win the first set.

Curren then came back and won the second set on the tiebreak. Game on! Early in the third set he looked more likely to win. He broke early, and I started to shout and scream, and lose my focus a little. He began to read my serve, his backhand return was working well, and a break up should have meant the set was his. I wasn't out of it, but things were looking ominous for me.

But then I broke him back for 4-4, and the momentum switched back to me. Finals are often won and lost on waves – if you're on top of the wave you have to ride it because it means you're up, but if you fall down you have to stop the fall. We call

Right: **I felt so good on grass that even in my first Wimbledon final at just 17 I was playing volleys like this one with perfect balance.**

it 'stopping the bleeding', and I had to stop the bleeding before the wound got too big to recover from. Breaking back for 4-4 stopped the bleeding, and once that happened there was an emotional switch. After that, when I won a big point, I started my little shuffle of satisfaction, and that was also something no-one had done before. Some people felt I was getting into my opponent's face, but I wasn't doing it to get at him, it was just as an expression of how I felt in that crucial moment. I was a boy who was excited.

So the wave was with me, but whether I kept riding the wave or fell off it would be determined by who won the third set. I had a set point at 5-4 and three more at 6-5, in fact the three at 6-5 were all second serves but I couldn't make any of them. So when he held serve for 6-6 to take us into another tiebreak, the momentum could have swung back to him. This is the kind of situation where one point, one stroke of luck, even one bad call (and we didn't have Hawk-Eye then) could decide the whole match.

The statistical records show that I won the tiebreak 7-3, but the numbers don't tell the story. The two crucial points were the second and third. On both of them, I made him play an extra volley, and he missed both on the backhand. When we changed ends after six points, I had won all six of them. He then went on to win three, but the damage had been done.

The momentum from the tiebreak allowed me to break him in the first game of the fourth set. At that point I sat down and said 'Five more service games'. I literally thought 'five more times holding serve'. It didn't put pressure on me – it helped me focus. That was my mindset when I came out to serve at 2-1, 3-2, 4-3. Then at 5-4 I felt the rush. I felt nervous for the first time, as I saw everybody screaming. I put a towel over my head and thought 'Oh my God'.

The umpire calls 'Time'. I walk out to receive the balls. *Four more points*. The screaming is almost unbearably loud. I try to bounce the ball and can hardly do it because it seems to stick to my hand. I start with a double fault. 0-15. *Still four more points*. I then put in a couple of good serves. 30-15. I then miss a first serve – what do I do with my second serve? I decide I can't play safe and for me not playing safe means I have to go for it, it's my way of expressing myself. So I go for a big second serve and it pays off. 40-15. *Two championship points*. More screaming. I prepare to serve but have to break off my service motion. The ball is barely leaving my left hand. An ace would do it, but I miss the first serve. Second serve; go for it – another double fault! 40-30.

I then close my eyes, and say a quiet prayer: 'God, give me one more point, just one more point'. I was raised a Roman Catholic, I took my first communion when I was 10 – I think there's a connection, I connect myself with a higher being, whatever His name is, but I believe in a god, I believe there's something greater than us. So I have this conversation with Him, He is the only guy I can talk to at this moment – no-one else will listen to me, so I have to get some inspiration from Him, and some peacefulness and quiet. I serve to the backhand, Kevin nets his return, and that's it – just as I'd imagined in my daydream the night before.

As I walked to the net I felt that my life had now changed. As I shook his hand, I felt this was a new beginning. It wasn't a feeling I'd known before.

I went through the formalities – shaking the umpire's hand, shaking the referee's hand, receiving the trophy, lifting the trophy, the lap of honour – and I saw people staring at me, in disbelief and in awe. I just couldn't believe what I'd done. I saw the president of West Germany, Richard von Weizsäcker, in the front row of a full Royal Box. My parents and sister had only flown in for the semi-final, no earlier, and I remember going back to the locker room and hugging them all. They looked at me in disbelief, as if they were saying 'You can't be our son'. And at that moment I felt whatever I left behind I left for good.

The media obligations took longer than the match. Then there was the champions' dinner, and I'd been told the men's champion had to dance with the women's champion. I thought I'd have to have the first dance with Martina Navratilova, and I couldn't dance. They'd actually abolished that tradition a few years before, but I didn't know, and Ţiriac was happy to string me along for a while, making me think I had to dance with Martina. When I found out I didn't I was relieved, but I still had other things to worry about. I didn't have a dinner jacket, I couldn't even tie a tie – I was simply not prepared, it hadn't been part of the plan to think about what would happen after the match. We went back to the Gloucester and I tried on a couple of tuxedos, it was only about the second time I'd worn one.

At about nine o'clock that evening, we walked into the Savoy. Everyone stood up, but funnily enough it didn't feel odd for me. I walked in there and felt I belonged – I'd won the tournament, so it was appropriate.

I had to make a speech but I kept it very short. I had no alcohol, a sip of champagne maybe – I was 17, I just didn't drink at all. At one stage the chairman of the club, Buzzer Hadingham, and his wife came up to where I was sitting with my parents. Buzzer spoke very good German, but his wife didn't. As they approached our table, I stood up, which prompted Mrs Lois Hadingham to look at my mother and exclaim 'Oh what a tall boy he is. What is he – six-two, six-three?' My mother's English was rather limited then, and she totally mistook the question. 'Oh no,' she said, '6-3, 6-7, 7-6, 6-4!' (it was the score by which I'd won the final!).

Talk to people who win their first major today, and they'll tell you they're lucky to get any sleep on the first night – there are celebrations until the small hours, and then a round of press, TV interviews and photo shoots in the morning. We just went back to the Gloucester. I slept pretty well – I can't remember for how long – and at around noon we flew out of London.

A day or two later, it emerged that my father had organised a reception with the mayor of Leimen. He said everyone wanted to see me, and to celebrate with me. That was the last thing I wanted but my father said I had to do it, it was his pride, and Ţiriac supported him. So a week after the final we had this open-topped Mercedes, like the Popemobile, and 30,000 or 40,000 people lined the streets as I drove through Leimen, including through my old neighbourhood. People who had known me for 17½ years were all of a sudden screaming my name, perhaps because they knew I was gone as the boy from their small town. It was strange; it felt very odd for me to get this much adulation. I felt awkward and didn't feel it was right – I was intimidated by it.

We went to the tennis club and a schoolmate of mine, Andreas, asked security if we could get in, and when the security guard was a bit suspicious, Andreas said 'Look, it's Boris Becker!' So the guy opened the gates, but I said quietly to my friend, 'Andi, just relax! I'm the same guy. I've won a tournament, but I haven't changed the world.' But he couldn't believe it. And that's when I got the physical evidence that people had changed. This was the feeling I'd had at match point – I got goosebumps, a feeling that something was different. A week later I had found out what.

The postscript to my Wimbledon triumph was provided by Erich Fritsch, the principal from the Helmholtz grammar school. I saw him on the parade, he came to the tennis club, and he asked me if we could have a quick chat. We talked for about 10 minutes, but his main line of conversation was whether I was really sure about a career as a tennis professional or whether I mightn't be better off going back to school. 'Herr Fritsch,' I said, 'I've just won Wimbledon! I realise something can still happen, but...'

'So you're not coming back?' he replied. 'I just have to hear it officially.'

'No,' I said, 'I'm not coming back.'

***Right:* I saw people staring at me, in disbelief and in awe.**

Chapter 4

Repeating and Losing (1986–87)

'The Re-education of Boris Becker'

ellesse
BASF

After a big tournament like Wimbledon, you go home. But where was home now? Where did I live? I'd moved to Monaco at 16 in a flat set up by Ion Ţiriac, but my parents still lived in Leimen.

My first destination after winning Wimbledon was Monte Carlo. When I asked Ţiriac about this, he said, 'I have to educate you now. Your life will never be the same…'

So for one week we stayed at the Old Beach Hotel in Monte Carlo. My apartment was very small, and Ţiriac wanted to be with me and explain what had just happened. And in that week it hit me.

One of my favourite albums ever was *The Miseducation of Lauryn Hill*. Hill wrote it in the late 1990s, and it refers back to problems in her group The Fugees and with her pregnancy. Looking back, what Ţiriac did in the couple of weeks after I won Wimbledon in 1985 could be termed 'The Re-education of Boris Becker'.

He explained in great detail what it would mean. The clothes I should wear – which shoes, which belt, shirts: blue, black, grey. He really gave me the whole lowdown. If you go to the Hôtel de Paris, you can't go in jeans and sneakers. If you go to a function you need to put on a tie, so he taught me how to tie a tie. Not that my father hadn't taught me, but I was a teenager, I didn't need to know how to tie a tie – my four-year-old who's growing up in England knows how to tie a tie because it's part of his school uniform.

Ţiriac drummed into me that there are a lot of dangers in being young, rich and famous. Girls will come, they'll tell you anything, be careful when you go to night clubs, what they put in your drinks. I said I didn't drink – he said it doesn't matter; they can put things in your water. Be careful with any girl you speak to, just open your eyes. You have great parents, they've

***Left:* Me, with my mother Elvira, sister Sabine, and father Karl-Heinz after winning Wimbledon in 1985.**

brought you up to be smart and self-reliant, but now it's different. People know that you've made a lot of money, and you'll make a lot more money – you're 17, you're the golden ticket for so many. And he repeated that sentence every day until it was embedded in my consciousness. You laugh at first, you don't take it seriously, but then you go out with him, and you realise what he's trying to say. You see a girl who a month ago couldn't be bothered to turn round, and now she's asking you to go out with her. So by my own experience I realised how people had changed towards me. I'd been living in Monte Carlo before Wimbledon, so it wasn't the first time I'd been to Jimmy's Bar, but it was the first time everyone at Jimmy's Bar wanted to come to my table.

It was only after a week of this 're-education' that I was able to spend some time at home with my family. And thankfully I found two people who hadn't changed: my mother and sister. They have never changed. My father was rather taken by the whole phenomenon, he was very proud of his boy; we had to calm him down sometimes, stop him from parading me too much and arranging too many interviews. My mother and sister were always cool – in fact my foundation right up to today has been the most loving and normal mother and sister. Through thick and thin they have been totally down-to-earth. They were happy and they celebrated my successes with me, but to them I'm still young Boris, and I'm so grateful for that.

The 11½ months between the two Wimbledons felt quite rough, but looking back they weren't that bad. I wasn't winning every tournament, which was to be expected, but everyone had a field day, saying my Wimbledon success was a flash in the pan – that I was famous for 15 minutes, never going to win another Grand Slam, should have lost to Nyström, should have lost to Mayotte, etc. Who was I to prove them wrong? I did win Cincinnati that summer; I also lost early in the US Open. I played OK and reached the final of the Masters in New York, where I lost to Ivan Lendl. All of which isn't bad for a 17-year-old – it would be considered a fantastic achievement today – but people were sort of expecting the summer of 1985 to repeat itself every month, and that was never going to happen.

There's another aspect that I think people find hard to understand, maybe it even seems ungrateful on my part: I think I'd have been a better player if I hadn't won Wimbledon at 17. I think it put me in a golden ball of repeating that performance over and over again, and it didn't give me the freedom or time to explore new things in tennis. I explored a bit later, but I think the Wimbledon win in 1985 stopped my development for two years. I wanted to win another Grand Slam and to play like that because I'd won like that, instead of working on my backcourt game, getting better on the backhand, improving my footwork, and just trying more things out. I was trapped by my own success. It's difficult to say whether I'd have won more majors if my breakthrough had come later, but I know I relied too long just on my serve, and you can't do that. It was too risky, but I was too methodical – it was serve and power, instead of a lesser serve, crafting the point, and working on the volley a bit more. I felt I missed out on a couple of years of exploration.

The main focus for the rest of 1985 was on team tennis, because West Germany had four home Davis Cup ties that year and reached the final. The enormity of what my Wimbledon title meant at home hit me when I flew to Hamburg for our Davis Cup quarter-final against the USA, four weeks after Wimbledon. When we beat Spain in the small southern town of Sindelfingen in April, we'd felt the buzz with three or four thousand spectators, but the stadium wasn't completely full. For the quarter-final, Hamburg's Rothenbaum stadium was packed with 12,000 people on all three days, and the buzz was just amazing. It was the first time Germany realised through its own experience that there was an international German sports star in tennis. We'd never had such amazing publicity: the weather was rainy, as usual for Hamburg, but the crowds still came out.

Above: **I returned to Leimen to celebrate winning my first Wimbledon in July 1985. They wanted to name the indoor courts after me..**

It wasn't the football season, so all the focus was on tennis, and the tie went to a live fifth match.

We should have won in two days, but Andreas Maurer and I lost the doubles 7-5 in the fifth set, and in the live fifth match I beat Aaron Krickstein 6-2, 6-2, 6-1. That made the last German who knew nothing about tennis realise that, for some reason, this Becker guy was the most popular person in the whole country.

The momentum continued in Frankfurt for the semi-final in October against Czechoslovakia. There was a marathon match between Michael Westphal and Tomas Smid on the first day, remembered by many for the carpet surface peeling away from the stone floor after Westphal came to the net for a volley. But once he had won that match, 15-13 in the fifth, we were away, and we won 5-0.

That gave us a home final the week before Christmas, which they staged in the Olympiahalle, the massive indoor arena built for the 1972 Munich Olympics. It had never been used for tennis before, and it was even bigger than Hamburg, with nearly 15,000 spectators, and sold out. The remarkable thing was that it clashed with the middle of the football season, but it still sold out – the whole country was watching. The biggest television sport show at the time was *Das Aktuelle Sportstudio*, a live Saturday night review of the day's sport with highlights and studio chat, and after every match we were interviewed in their live studio. It was the first time a tennis event had been televised in such a major fashion. We lost the final to the mighty Swedes because Maurer and I were outclassed in the doubles by Nyström and Wilander, but that weekend put tennis properly on the map in Germany and indirectly was a massive investment for me in my future playing career.

But that brought pressures. By the end of the year I'd established myself as a top five player, yet everybody expected me to shoot to No. 1 overnight, at least that's how it felt to me (and I had certain expectations as well). I felt I was good, but something was missing. It was only later that I realised what it was: I needed to win Wimbledon a second time, just to show the world that the first was no fluke.

Once again, the key to winning Wimbledon came in a moment of crisis. I didn't question whether I would make it as a professional as I'd already done that, nor was I ready to quit the way I was in South Africa in November 1984. But I did tell my coach and manager to stop coaching me. And that was just two weeks before Wimbledon began.

The first couple of months of 1986 were OK, but then I had a stretch in which I always seemed to lose in the quarter-finals. There were four or five tournaments, including the French Open and the clay court tournaments. I even lost in the quarters in Queen's and failed to defend my first title. I lost to Tim Mayotte, and that was when I hit crisis point. It's hard to define what it was exactly – I wasn't on the verge of burnout, but I felt I was working in ways I didn't believe in and in directions I didn't believe in. I was listening a lot to Ţiriac and Bosch, but with all the quarter-final defeats I wondered if I was maybe listening to them too much.

After I lost to Mayotte at Queen's, I said 'Listen guys, let's sit down. I've got to change. I'm not going to win Wimbledon like this. I've listened to you, I've been an animal in practice, I've done more than you've asked me, but something's not clicking any more. I need to rediscover my instinct, my natural aggressiveness, my sense of going for my shots under pressure.' So I asked them to say nothing to me about tennis over the next two weeks. I said they could drive me to the courts, they could pick up the balls in practice, but I didn't want any input about tennis. I said if I was wrong, then so be it, they could then say they were right, but I wanted the opportunity to do what I believed was right.

So you have an 18-year-old telling his coach not to coach him, and his manager, a former top player and proven coach, not to give any tennis input either! That put me under pressure in my practice week. I felt good about what I'd said; in fact I felt I should probably have said it two months earlier, but the moment just hadn't been right. I felt released, in control again, I was making decisions about how I wanted to practise and play, and so forth. I had a heightened awareness. Obviously everyone thought I was mad – after all, nobody had ever won Wimbledon at that age before me, let alone defended it.

As I walked out on to Centre Court at 2pm on the first Monday as the defending champion, it felt good to be back. But I actually felt ready to close the chapter of being the 17-year-old Wimbledon champion. 'This is now it,' I thought. 'Enough waiting, enough of whether I could do it or not – let's play!' And in retrospect it was probably my best Wimbledon ever. The type of tennis I played, the way I focused, the way I played with sheer aggression and single-mindedness to win – that was probably me at my very best.

The draw wasn't that easy but it started with Eduardo Bengoechea, which was OK because like many Argentineans he wasn't great on grass, and I went through him in straight sets. Tom Gullikson was harder but I beat him in straight too, and then I had a tough match in the third round against Paul McNamee in which I dropped my first set. That set me up to play Mikael Pernfors in the round of the last 16 on No. 2 Court. Pernfors had beaten me in the quarters at the French in what was his breakthrough tournament – he had gone on to reach the final of the French and was the new rising star. It was after I beat him in straight sets that Ţiriac and Bosch finally asked to say something to me. They said 'Keep on going – we've got the message. Do what you do; this is amazing. Just keep it up.' That was very soothing, it gave me a good sense that they understood what I had to go through. I felt my team was back: my team believed in my leadership again.

So I was back in the quarter-finals, and people finally began to take seriously the idea that I might defend my title. There were a few differences to the previous year, like the fact that I'd changed hotels. Despite the superstition of wanting to stay in the same hotel in which I'd won the title, the Gloucester was too busy. It was the players' hotel and I wanted some privacy. I liked the neighbourhood but wanted a smaller hotel nearby, so we stayed in the Londonderry (now the Metropolitan). But we still had dinner at San Lorenzo's, I still had my same meal every night of T-bone steak with pasta, and I was still under the radar.

My quarter-final opponent was someone I genuinely feared. Miloslav Mecir was a tough adversary for me, because he had

Right: **The type of tennis I played, the way I focused, the way I played with sheer aggression. I had a single-mindedness to win.**

Above: **I chat with Ion Ţiriac (*right*) and Günther Bosch (*left*).**

a good backhand and he returned very well. But I was in my favourite second-match-on-Centre slot, and I defeated him by the near-identical score with which I'd beaten Pernfors in the last round. I was incredibly determined.

With McEnroe taking a sabbatical and Connors having lost early, I felt very confident from the semis onwards. I was playing Henri Leconte, who I knew well and had beaten the previous year. I dropped the third set against him on the tiebreak, but I was feeling so good after the first two sets against Henri. I had to show him first that I was here to win, because the longer we played the better he got and those first two sets were crucial. It meant I could afford to lose the third and still be OK, and I wrapped it up comfortably in the fourth.

The victory put me into the final against Ivan Lendl. Most of the focus was on him. He had won the French and US Opens, but this was the one he wanted. He was world No. 1, he'd just won the French Open, and he was doing everything that was humanly possible to become the champion of Wimbledon.

That was his agenda, but I had mine. I felt that the final was a big chance for me to truly establish myself as a top tennis player. I knew even then that I had to win to show it hadn't been an accident the previous year. Up to the final, I was in a tunnel – my only thought was 'who's next?' – but when it comes to the final you begin to think a bit more. And I realised this was the day I had to do it. Winning the final would give me peace of mind. It would give me a proper belief and understanding that I'm one of the best tennis players in the world, that I can trust myself no matter what, that I can cope with pressure, and I'm here to stay around for a long time.

For some reason, on grass and in Slams, I felt good against Ivan. He was serving and volleying all the time, which wasn't his natural game, and his backhand return wasn't so good, so I had a target to aim for, which gave me a bit of a safety net. And in this final I was the more experienced – I may have been eight years younger than him, but I'd won a Wimbledon title and this was his first final.

The first two sets were all me. I broke him in each set and after barely an hour I was two sets up. But then he came back in the third when my level dropped. He should have won the third set – he was 4-1 up in games, and had three set points at 0-40 on my serve at 4-5. I expected him to win the third set, I was fully prepared to play four sets, and for that reason I kept coming to the net. I knew that's how I had to play, regardless of the score, and my attitude of not being afraid made him uncomfortable. I saved the set points, and when I got back to 5-5 there was a switch of momentum. He backed off a bit, I pushed forward, and I broke him for 6-5.

So here, a year after my nervous final game against Curren, I was serving for a victory that would be less of a shock but would be worth more to me. And on the second point of that final game, I had a chance to stamp my mark on Wimbledon's history. I served out wide to the backhand, came to the net, and volleyed his return into the forehand corner. He raced across his baseline and went for a forehand passing shot down the line. I dived for it, but it hit the tape and dropped over. At the moment it hit the net cord I was airborne and horizontal. The fact that the ball dropped over should have finished me, but it dropped close enough to me that I could play a crosscourt winner into the open court while still on the ground. I was so elated I did my shuffle and gestured in triumph with my arms. A couple of minutes later I served out the victory. It was one of the top three matches of my entire playing career.

That relief, that celebration, that joy was by far the biggest I've had in my life. It was by far the most emotional I've been, but in a very quiet way.

I think I can honestly say that every big match I had after that, every very important tennis match, every crossroads, every identity crisis – I would always look back to Wimbledon 1986

Above: **The satisfaction of winning my second Wimbledon was one of the most empowering feelings in my entire career.**

and say 'If I can do that at 18, I can do it at 25, 27, whenever. When push came to shove, I didn't run away.' That was the red line of understanding throughout my tennis career and probably afterwards – I can trust myself.

My immediate feeling on winning was 'I know who I am now'. Tennis was always a metaphor for my personal struggles – if I was struggling in my private life, you'd see it on the tennis court, and if I wasn't, you'd see that too. Leading up to Wimbledon I was struggling with my identity – who am I, who do I trust, where do I go after winning Wimbledon at 17? I couldn't get a bigger high than that, so I felt a little confused and unsure of myself. That changed over those 14 days in 1986.

As the weeks and months passed, I realised just how significant that victory had been. I had really rediscovered what made me strong in the first place, this determination, this controlled aggression, this single-mindedness, focusing on one goal and one goal only: the love of competition and putting it on the line. Ivan had been the right opponent – he was No. 1 in the world, which is where I wanted to be one day. I knew that if I played well I could beat him. Obviously if I didn't play well I'd lose, but in matches with Pete Sampras later on I knew that even if I played well he could still beat me, and with Agassi if he was returning well I'd have trouble. But in 1986, I felt that if I was playing well on grass, I was tough to beat.

I had also lain to rest the pressure of being Wimbledon champion at 17. That was an amazing triumph, but I think it led me to try to please people too much. I was trying to fit into a mould that was created for me as the youngest Wimbledon champion; I felt I had to behave a certain way and say certain things and look a certain way. Winning Wimbledon a second time made me feel that I could act according to my truth, that I have to stay true to my beliefs. Those beliefs may not be right for everyone, but they're right for me. I felt some of my sense of self was taken away by having won Wimbledon at 17, and I'd won it back by winning Wimbledon at 18.

***Right:* I serve during a match at the 1986 French Open.**

Once again my former school principal had the last word, but this time it was a joke. That summer was the end of the two-year period in which he was holding open my schooling. There was no parade in Leimen this time, so he contacted my mother just after my second Wimbledon title, saying with a twinkle in his eye, 'I take it he's not coming back?'

I went to Wimbledon in 1987 having never lost a main draw match by losing the final point. My first main draw was 1984 when I'd been carried off on a stretcher, and I'd won the title in 1985 and 86. To some I was invincible, but not to me. And that's the reason behind the quote I'm probably best known for in the first part of my tennis career.

I went on a run of good results after Wimbledon in 1986. I won Toronto; I was a semi-finalist at the US Open; I won two or three indoor tournaments in the autumn, reached the Masters final, and finished the year at No. 2 in the world. I felt the door had opened and I was where I should be. I carried this on into 1987 until the French Open when I reached the semis. I'd reached the final in Monte Carlo (I was good on clay then!), and I was close to the No. 1 ranking – Lendl was just a few points ahead.

Then Wimbledon came. I felt the pressure was off, because I'd proved myself at other tournaments. I was a little tired because I'd played so much leading up to Wimbledon, but not seriously tired, just a bit weary. I had my traditional defending champion's opener on Centre Court, in which I beat Karel Novacek in straight sets. That victory set up a second round match against Peter Doohan, an Australian ranked 70 but who had won a title and reached a couple of finals on grass in Australia, so he was not to be underestimated. He won the first set on the tiebreak, but I broke him in the second for one set all. At that point

I looked and felt in control, but he lifted his level and I couldn't pick up the pressure. I lost fair and square in four sets.

I accepted the defeat. I felt it was part of the give-and-take of sport – if I was happy to win the tournament in 1986, then I had to be willing to accept the loss in 1987. I was still very much a major player in world tennis, even if I dropped from second to fourth in the rankings, and I felt I was challenging for the No. 1 spot on all surfaces.

So it was totally natural in one of my post-match interviews – it was live on the BBC – that I said, 'I've lost a tennis match, I haven't lost a war – nobody was killed.' This had an extraordinary resonance, but I didn't mean it to. As tennis players we understand better than most how close so many matches are. Literally a single point can make the difference between winning and losing – look at my matches with Nyström and Mayotte in 1985 – so we don't kid ourselves, even if we sometimes try to tell the world that our victory was never in doubt; it's very much in doubt most of the time. I wanted to put my defeat in perspective. I think journalists often don't give enough credit to the loser, and the winner gets too much glory without people understanding that the match could have gone either way. The result doesn't mean one player is better than

the other; just that one beat the other on the day. I was trying to say: please don't put me on a pedestal when I win because I could have lost, and please don't now put me in the cellar and throw me to the lions when I lose to a very talented Australian player who happened to be better that day. I was 19, and at that age you don't think about it, it just comes out. I didn't want to be the hamster in the wheel, so I said what I felt because I really meant it, but it wasn't a prepared comment or meant to be a big philosophical statement.

There was perhaps another reason for my defeat to Doohan: I was slightly less driven for Wimbledon. I had been striving to become a complete player on all surfaces, and I wanted to win other major titles, so Wimbledon wasn't the most important tournament for me any more because I knew I could win there.

My first proper defeat was also a relief. After the 1985 win the phenomenon was created, the 'Wunderkind', 'the 17-year-old Leimener', and that was the biggest burden, living up to the expectation every time I went anywhere. I'm not complaining – the alternative would have been to lose early in the 1985 tournament – but the run at Wimbledon had created an aura that wasn't always helpful to me. With the loss to Doohan, some of that aura disappeared. It was like saying there are no miracles in this world, and I could mind my own business again. I was talented, I was one of the top players, but I wasn't a 'Wunderkind', I wasn't the kid who was never going to lose at Wimbledon, the guy who was going to break Borg's record of five successive titles. That was never my intention. I wanted to be the best player in the world and Wimbledon was part of the journey, but it wasn't the only tournament I wanted to win. Obviously I wanted to beat Doohan, I didn't go into the match wanting to lose, but I accepted it afterwards as part of the big jigsaw puzzle of where I needed to be.

By then I had established the foundations for the rest of my career. German television was now broadcasting all the matches. The stardom I reached, particularly in Germany, was mind-blowing – even though I lost in the second round, it was headline news. I had established myself, and I had established the interest in tennis in my home country.

I knew I had a few weaknesses, I needed to improve my game, and soon after Wimbledon I broke up with my long time coach Günther Bosch. To some this was a major story, and it was sad in a way to split from the guy who had coached me during my two Wimbledon titles. But it was all part of my personal evolution. I felt, tennis-wise, I needed a bit more than what Günther was giving me and it was a natural time for a break. I didn't take on a new coach immediately; I looked around for a few months, and then took on Bob Brett.

Despite my defeat at Wimbledon, by the middle of 1987 I felt good. I wasn't thinking any more about whether I belonged because I did, I wasn't thinking any more about whether this was something I wanted to do because I did. I just wanted to be a good tennis player. I felt very comfortable in the tennis world, and I accepted the fact that you do lose sometimes, for whatever reason, and that's OK as long as you win more than you lose. My identity was clear: I was confident, I was a young man with few doubts, my life was good, I wasn't tormented by the devil, I wasn't having sleepless nights, I was with a nice girlfriend, and I was up for the challenge of getting better as a tennis player. Everything was very much in place for the next couple of years.

The All England Club

Needless to say, the All England Lawn Tennis and Croquet Club has a massive place in my consciousness. It was the scene of the triumph that launched my career, and I will always have a soft spot for it. I'm genuinely fond of the place, more so than in the early years of my playing career.

In some ways, it's a little strange to have a top-level global sporting event run by a private club, but that's what it is: a private club. Forty years ago that was normal. The US Open was held at the private Westside Tennis Club at Forest Hills until the US Tennis Association built its own national tennis centre at Flushing Meadows in 1978; and the Australian Open was played at the private Kooyong Club in the outer suburbs of Melbourne until 1987, when it moved to the purpose-built, city centre Melbourne Park in 1988. You might think Wimbledon ought to have made the same move, but by a very clever balancing act of maintaining tradition on the surface and modernising behind the scenes, it has preserved its sense of class while also keeping up with the times.

I think the committee and staff of the All England Club have done an incredible job of moving with the times, of keeping the tradition yet updating themselves every couple of years with things like the roof, the quality of the courts, the quality of the service, and most importantly, the branding. The reason they are the premier tournament in the world is that they have understood the value of Wimbledon and they've been most professional about their tournament, probably more than any other tournament. History helps, but they have found a way of protecting it, and in this respect, what they do is a masterclass.

What you see on the television or when you visit Wimbledon is the club in 'Championships' mode. For the other 50 weeks of the year, it is a club like most other tennis clubs. It has 19 grass courts, eight North American clay courts, and five indoor courts. You have members, and they play when they can. They are provided with tennis balls and even their towels if they shower after a match. There are club matches, in which the club competes against other clubs in local leagues. There is a social scene too – you can drop in for Sunday lunch, and you can use the bar. But there is a strict dress code: if you want to play on any of the courts (even the indoor ones) you have to wear all-white just like during the Championships, and if you want to eat in the bar or restaurant, gentlemen have to wear a jacket and tie, with the ladies dressing to an equivalent level of smartness. (And they are 'gentlemen' and 'ladies' at Wimbledon, not 'men' and 'women'.) The old tea room in the clubhouse is now the club room and is more relaxed – you can get food and drinks up to 8pm, and you can go there in your tennis clothes.

There are two ways of becoming a member of the club. One is to apply for membership – you fill in a form, find a proposer and five seconders from among the existing members, all of who cannot propose or second more than two new members per year. You can often wait 10–15 years to become a temporary member, and then after another five years or so you are

Centre Court - South West Hall

proposed for full membership. The other way is to win one of the Wimbledon singles titles. So yes, I'm a member because I won the gentleman's singles, not because I applied and waited 20 years. A few people are fast-tracked for membership – people who have given a lot of time and money to the sport of tennis are encouraged to apply (a good example is the singer and tennis fan Cliff Richard), plus those who have represented their country or their county. There's also a strong link to Oxford and Cambridge – the current chairman Philip Brook was the captain of the Cambridge University team when he was a student, and his predecessor Tim Phillips played for Oxford University.

Only recently did I learn that there are just 500 members of the All England Club. And if you think they are all millionaires, you're wrong. Some of them are, but you don't have to be a millionaire to be a member – you just have to be approved. Annual membership costs £100, which tells you that how much money you have isn't important. Having said that, one of the members is the former head of the Bank of England, so money does play its part in a roundabout way.

Most former singles champions enjoy their membership but few of them make much use of it, and although I live locally, I'm not that different. It's perhaps a real irony that I drive past the All England Club every single day when I go to my office in the

***Left:* I know that feeling. Novak celebrates with the trophy on the clubhouse balcony after winning the Wimbledon Men's Singles title.**

city of London. I do go occasionally to the club, but not often – the chairman is always asking me to come, and maybe I should go there more often, but something stops me. I go into Centre Court sometimes, or I go to the lounge, but I seldom play there. I suppose I want to protect my memories and not make it an everyday part of my life.

My relationship with the club was not always so comfortable. I used to have difficulties with the tradition. As a youngster you're more rebellious – I didn't want to understand some of the rules, I didn't want to obey them all. It took me a long time to work out why everyone had to wear white, why they had to bow in front of the Royal Box, why *this* and why *that*.

Over the years I've come to understand why it's like that, and I respect it so much more now than I did when I was playing. Both Wimbledon and I have matured. During the 1989 Championships, after I'd been warned for wearing a Fila shirt that didn't meet the club's 'predominantly white' rule (see page 125), I had a chat with the German press, and admitted I was irritated with some of the tradition and stuffiness. I complained that they were so strict they'd throw you off the court if you wore blue underpants, and it made headlines. I was a boy then, and I became a man in the intervening years, so some of my views then are not necessarily views I'd subscribe to now.

Maybe one day I'll make myself available for a couple of team matches, but I wouldn't want to do that without being properly prepared. And would I get any fun out of it? – I'm not sure I would. The problem is that after two hip replacements, two ankle operations and a whole range of other injuries, I don't move very well these days. I certainly don't want to play singles. My glory days are over, even if people still have this image of a 25-year-old serving at high speed and throwing himself around. But I can still hit the ball, I hit with Novak Djokovic in practice sessions, so you never know, I might offer myself for a doubles match or two. It would be quite fun to turn up and watch the opposition's reaction when they see who they're playing against. Just don't tell them I can't run for the ball any more.

Right: **Two great arenas – No. 1 Court and Centre Court at Wimbledon, just before they added the roof!**

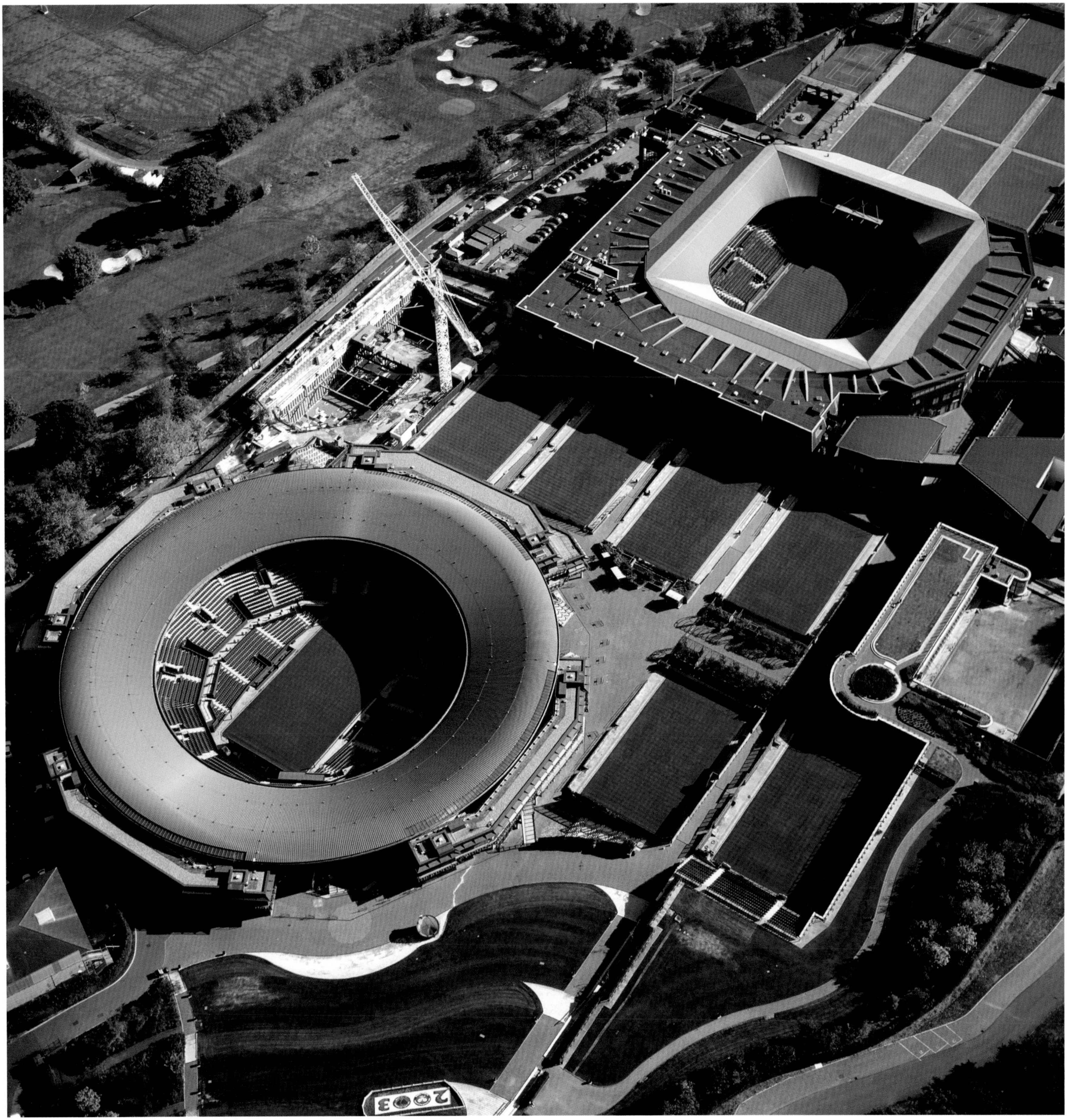

Chapter 5

Six finals in seven years (1988–91)

'Just testing the boundaries.'

FILA
SergioTacchini

Having won two Wimbledon titles at 18 – which, let's face it, no-one had done before or has done since – it's very easy to look back on my haul of three Wimbledon titles and six Slams in total as a bit of a disappointment. I share some of that disappointment, but I think you need to see the bigger picture. I reached six Wimbledon finals in seven years, and even in the three years after 1991 when I concentrated more on my private life I still reached one quarter-final and two semis. That's not bad going.

The period 1988–91 was the peak of the Becker-Edberg rivalry. Stefan and I played three successive Wimbledon finals, and it should have been four but for Michael Stich hitting the form of his life and beating Edberg in the 1991 semi-finals (and even then Stefan didn't lose his serve). It was also the peak of my career, though if you look carefully you see the signs of a young man still trying to make sense of the world and his own place in it.

Looking back, there were two themes running through this period – one to do with me, the other to do with the health of tennis in general.

The sport today is terrific. We have a great generation of players, but one of the things we're missing is real tension between two characters in a top-level match. I think today's tennis can be a little too politically correct. The guys at the top are all competitors, they don't like losing any more than I did, but I wish we could see a little more of their rivalry and aggressiveness. I understand why they don't show too much – it's a family sport, kids are watching, and through their demeanour players have become household names and role models, unlike players such as McEnroe or Connors who may have been household names but weren't held up as examples. But I find it sometimes a little too fake, because we all know how much they want to win. It would add an extra dimension to the game if we could see more of the honest competitiveness and the drive and desire to win.

My quarter-final against Pat Cash at Wimbledon in 1988 was an example of the kind of match we lack today. Pat was a very aggressive competitor, and so was I. He was an Australian tennis prodigy who started playing well in his mid-teens, he represented Australia in the Davis Cup very early, and he'd been a semi-finalist at Wimbledon in 1984, so it was a logical step for him to win Wimbledon. He did that in 1987. Everyone expected him to win a lot more, so in 1988 he was one of the top players – the defending champion, runner-up at the Australian Open a few months earlier, and member of the elite. Now he came up against this other young, aggressive competitor from Germany, one with a very different family background and very different upbringing, and a rival for the accolade of 'the best on grass'. We're really good friends now, but back in the day Pat was not a popular face in the locker room because of his brashness and cockiness. I didn't care about that because I was similar, but you can see why our quarter-final was massively hyped – it

***Left:* Pat Cash and I are all smiles as we receive trophies from Princess Diana in 1988, but Diana's face sums up what Pat and I thought of each other!**

was the meeting of the champions of the last three years who didn't really like each other. He was 23, I was 20 and there were masses of teenagers in the crowd chanting our names.

The match was pretty one-sided, I beat him in straight sets, but that's not what it's remembered for. There was a little harmless incident in the second set which told the world about the 'needle' between us. By then I was a set and 4-1 up and he was upset about the way the match was going. I played a drop shot, he was physically very fit so he chased it down, but his momentum made him hit the net and roll over onto my side. I decided to have a bit of fun and roll over the net onto his side, and the crowd enjoyed it. I offered to shake hands with him as part of the fun, but he refused. At the next change of ends he muttered a few words that should not be repeated in polite society, words I told the press that he had taught me. And after the match he had this spiky bright red wig in the press conference. I think he was trying to get back at me.

After that we were proper rivals. When we played each other, it became one of those matches that we could do with seeing today – a match when two fiercely competitive guys go at each other not just during the match but before and after as well, creating a bit of a scene. It's good for ratings and interest in tennis. That stayed with us throughout our careers. Fortunately, I was always able to answer him not verbally but with my results – I won all our three matches on grass and only lost to him once.

So why don't players make more of their rivalry now? I'll give you one example from my era that might explain it. Michael Stich and I didn't particularly like each other, and we told the world about it. Like with Pat Cash, Michael and I are good friends now, but when we were rivals we were happy to admit that we weren't friends. It meant we were asked about it every single time we played each other, which was not only very wearing, but

***Right:* I changed my hair a lot in those days - in 1988 I had floppy hair.**

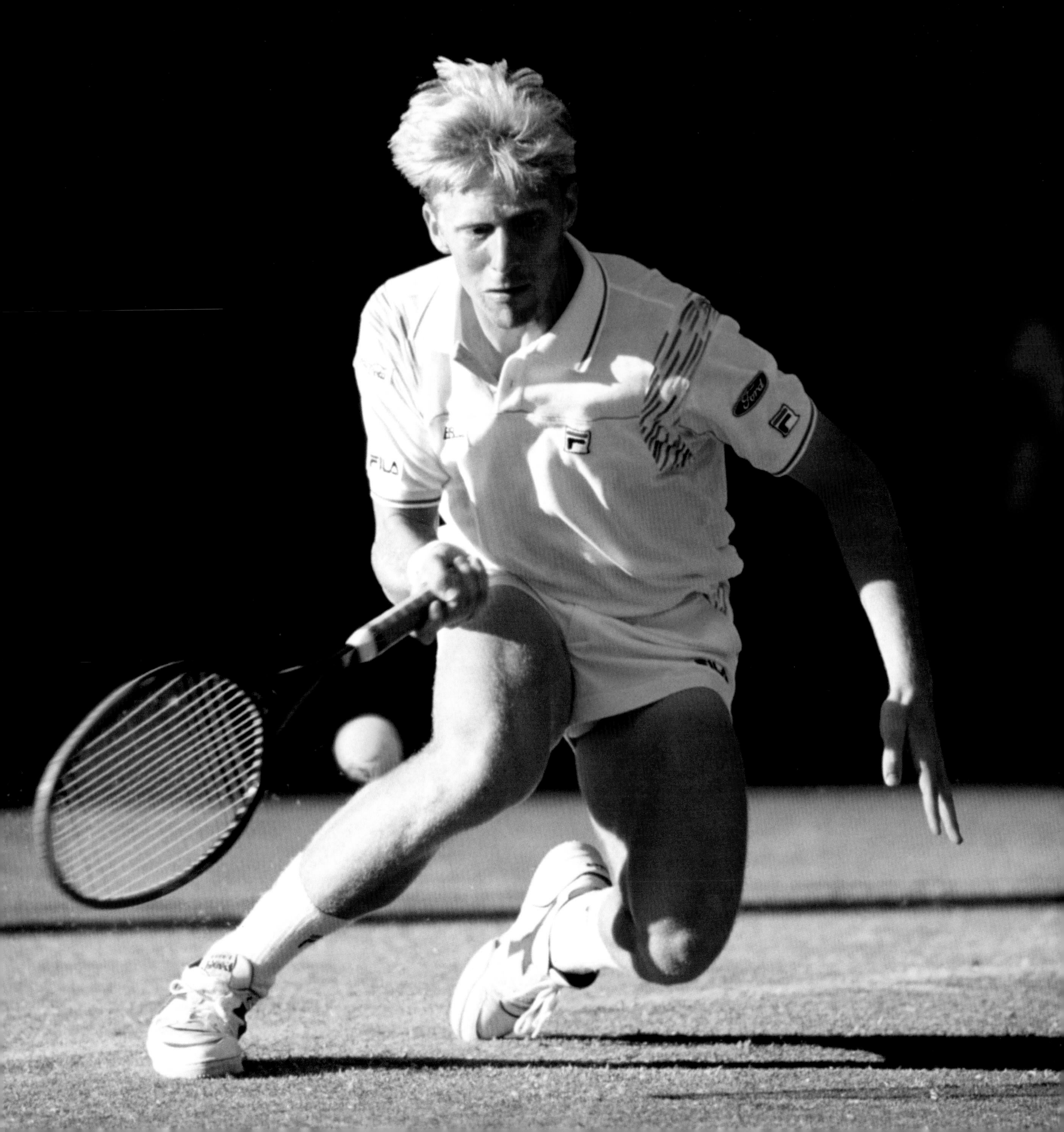
FILA

it made life complicated because our wives and girlfriends at the time couldn't get along either – that was almost the bigger problem for us. Yet the only reason we didn't like each other was because we didn't know each other and saw each other only as competitors and rivals. Eventually I told the media, 'Listen, I only have a couple of friends – I think that's natural, most people are like that – and Michael is not one of them. But that doesn't mean I hate him, it just means he isn't one of my close friends.' Yet throughout our whole careers people created difficulties for us, so I think it's easier, or less complicated, if today's top players sometimes don't tell the full truth.

One of the open secrets on today's tennis tour is that Roger Federer and Novak Djokovic don't particularly like each other. Like with Michael Stich and I, they don't hate each other, and they have tremendous mutual respect. But when Roger was at the top, Novak was the young challenger who irritated Roger by often calling for the trainer because of some illness, while Novak felt he had to break into the 'big two' of Federer and Nadal so used Roger's status as an incentive for him to be the underdog that crashes the establishment's party. It's therefore totally natural that they aren't close to each other, that they *respect* more than *like* each other.

So should these two role models be more openly aggressive? Is it good for tennis that they maintain this dignified respect that covers up for any antipathy?

***Left:* Back at Wimbledon in 1989 with a military haircut.**

To answer this, you need to ask who's to judge what is good for tennis and what's not good for tennis. Men's tennis is very popular; the ratings in most countries are higher now than they were 10 years ago. That's because of the characters we have – because of Federer, Nadal, Djokovic, Murray and others. But I believe we'd get higher ratings if we could see even more of their personalities, and if that means it becomes obvious that they don't really like each other, I don't think that would hurt tennis or their careers. Obviously they listen to what their advisers tell them, what's useful, correct, and sponsorship plays a role.

The reason Roger is one of the highest-paid athletes of all time is because he's liked by everybody. But think about this – you cannot possibly be liked by everybody or you have no character! Now I'm not saying Roger has no character because he clearly has. What I'm saying is that it's just an impossible image to portray, so why try? He makes good money out of his image, but would he make less if we saw a bit more of his true feelings? That's the way sport is at the moment, but I think it'll change, I think in five years time we'll find more characters, more personalities, let's call it more honesty. That doesn't mean you won't get contracts because you have passion and personality – it's something everyone wants.

At the end of 2014, I was asked to serve on an advisory board on how to make men's tennis more attractive. One of the things I want us to look at is the code of conduct, to see if we can relax it a little more. People occasionally put it to me that tennis is

more boring now than when I played and when I ask them why they say there are fewer characters. I reply that we have great characters, but it's true they don't show it as much because they can't, they get fined and there are microphones on the court that pick up every curse or utterance of frustration. As a result, it's very difficult to verbalise your frustration nowadays because everyone hears it and you go back to the locker room to face a fine of $10,000, $20,000 or even more. Thus they don't do it and it robs us of the chance to see some of the personality of the stars.

I accept it's a difficult problem to solve, because you don't want players setting a bad example to 10-year-olds. There's a fine line to be drawn. I think Novak and Rafa, in their passionate style, found a solution in cheering along with the crowd and clenching a fist, not necessarily towards the other guy, but just to support their own emotions. Andy Murray is honest, but in a negative way. I've never seen a guy – not even McEnroe – who commentates on every single point the way Murray does. It's mind-boggling how much he speaks to himself during a match, but I'd like to see more of that because the players have it in them. They should give it the fist or display something that shows spectators a particular point was important to them. I hope there is scope for us to relax the code of conduct so we see the personalities without turning them into bad examples for the next generation of tennis fans. I think it would add to the game.

The other theme of this period is my own image. If you look back at the highlights of Wimbledon 1988, you'll see me with quite long, floppy hair. If you look at me during 1989, my hair is much shorter, almost a military cut. By 1992 I had a beard. There's a reason for all that and it is reflected in where I was as a tennis player.

Left: **And in 1992 I had a beard.**

It was probably subconscious, but I was determined that I would never become a 'product'. I always felt I was my own man, I'm my own responsibility, I'm independent, I can pay my bills, I'm not beholden to anybody – and I was determined to have my own image, even if that meant changing my haircut every year. That was one of the physical statements I made throughout my whole career. I am my own man. I could have got a contract with a shaving or hair gel company, but that would have committed me to a certain look, and I wasn't willing to sign a contract that tied me to that. I want to be valued as a human being, as a successful sportsman, and not because I fit into an image or fashion.

I had marketing people, notably Ion Ţiriac, but he protected my innocence. He took the view 'Let Boris be Boris, he's going to win a lot more tournaments and a lot more money if he's allowed to be himself than if he feels he's become a product and has to do what you tell him. He has a good heart, a good soul, he's not a bad man, but he has to keep a degree of independence.' Ţiriac was very smart with that. I always felt I wanted to look myself in the mirror and know I'm not somebody else's product. I try to treat my family and friends with a lot of respect and a lot of love, and what I do professionally has to be consistent with my beliefs. I may have missed out on a contract or two, I may have made a mistake, but I'm more at peace today because of it.

This is an issue everyone has to confront at some point. I think I'm comfortable with myself today because I didn't just take every contract that came my way. And when I see other prodigies who were dubbed a 'Wunderkind' and how they were marketed – 30 years later they live a very different life than I do. That's an important message, especially to those who have been called a 'Wunderkind': take control of your own life as soon as possible, because it's the only one you have.

It's interesting that I never had a contract with the two biggest clothing companies, Adidas and Nike. As a German you'd think Adidas, as a German company, would be a logical choice for me, but a lot of athletes with Nike or Adidas become products, and I felt there was a danger in that. It's the same in football, basketball, even boxing – athletes are marketed in a very specific way, and you can easily become a sporting politician. I understand the attraction of the money, but it's dangerous for the young person because you can get to the point where you don't understand who you are any more. The danger is that you can lose your identity and your personality. I had a long-term contract with Puma, and you can see which personalities are signed by Puma – they're very different to the ones signed by Adidas and Nike. I've ended up coaching a player who's also with a smaller clothing company. I think that goes hand-in-hand with the personality I am, and with the people I like to hang out with.

Looking back, I had a bit of a thing about being used for marketing. Being such a high-profile figure, certain things I said were sometimes used for marketing purposes, all of which I never intended. For example, when Mercedes brought out the A-Klasse, they had a test to show the stability of the car when taking sharp corners and the company invited all the international motoring press to Sweden to see the A-Klasse car doing a sharp turn on a slippery surface and staying upright. And what happened? – the car rolled over! It was one of the worst moments in marketing. They wanted to show the A-Klasse was totally safe, and the car then did the exact opposite of what it was supposed to do. The marketing director in those days, Dieter Zetsche, who's now the big boss at Daimler, was chatting to me one day, saying what an embarrassment it was and saying the company was still working out how to react. At one point he asked me 'What was your strategy when you had a big loss?' And I replied 'I always learned a lot more from my losses than from my victories.' His eyes lit up. 'Great,' he said, 'that's the marketing campaign for our new A-Klasse.' I was honoured in a way, but I said that simply because I felt it. Obviously the

agencies that are paid for these slogans got all the credit, yet the slogan came from me.

Something similar happened with AOL. They were trying to show Germany how easy it is to get on to the internet. Fifteen years ago I didn't know a lot myself and I had a photo shoot all day with the mass media company; it was just not happening – whatever they asked me to say, it didn't sound credible. Eventually I asked the agency if I could just be myself for a bit, say what I'd say if I was on a computer for the first time. So I played around, and all of a sudden I just said 'Ich bin drin' ('I'm in'). In those days I was a bit of a playboy and the phrase had something of a double meaning, not just about getting 'in' to the internet. They said 'Yes, that's great!' I think the slogan won all the prizes for commercials, and again the agency took the credit, but the idea came from an instinctive moment I had because that was how I felt. These are examples where my positive instincts were used to commercialise a product, which I understand, but those are the reasons why I didn't want to become a product myself.

Having said that, there are also practical considerations, and it became clear at Wimbledon in 1988 that my hair was a bit too long at the front. So during my semi-final against Ivan Lendl, I took out a pair of scissors during a change of ends and cut a bit off my fringe. No mirror, I just cut a bit off so I could see better. I was also using my freedom and liberty – when I felt my hair was too long, I cut it. I wasn't going to a hairdresser or having a special look, I just did it.

Left: **My serve was always a big part of my game.**

That match against Lendl was my first against him at Wimbledon since I beat him in the final in 1986. And in a way nothing had changed. He had lost two successive finals – to me and Pat Cash – pretty much the same way, both in straight sets, and both with him having good leads but blowing them. He appeared not to have learned anything from those defeats, or maybe he wasn't capable of learning.

Lendl was all about control and calculation, but to win on grass, it's very difficult to calculate what exactly you have to do, and there are lots of factors you can't control. How can you control the weather? How can you control an unreliable bounce? Lendl liked maths – he liked to calculate everything, which is fine when it comes to working out how many times he had to cycle round the park, how many calories he had to eat, but grass court tennis is more about instincts, and naturally staying aggressive under pressure. That was his problem. That's why he never won Wimbledon. It's also why I never won the French – because on clay it's exactly the opposite: you have to be a lot more patient and calculating, and often you win through the other player's mistakes, whereas at Wimbledon you only win because of your winners. Lendl could never trust his instincts, and I knew that. I also knew that my style really bothered him, that not giving him time, attacking the backhand constantly, and taking a swing at his serve could unsettle him. On a surface

where there was lots he couldn't control, I didn't give him time to prepare the point.

He was coached at that time by Tony Roche. Roche had turned Ivan from a nearly-man to a Slam winner, but his way of playing on grass was to come to the net after every serve. That's fine when you have a big lefty serve like Roche did, but I don't think it was Lendl's best strategy. Before Lendl, Borg had won Wimbledon by playing a lot of points from the baseline, and Agassi later won it playing nearly all his points from the baseline. Yet Lendl was set on serving and volleying after every point. The problem was that his second serve often wasn't good enough, and he was often caught in no-man's land. I guess it was part of his strategy – he had to repeat his style as part of his calculations. It was easier for him to come to the net after every second serve than have to work out when he could come in and when not, and that was his downfall. Well, two finals and a few semis is not a *downfall*, but that's why he never won Wimbledon.

In the final against Edberg I was the clear favourite. I had lots of confidence having beaten Cash and Lendl, and I won the first set, even after losing the first three games. That strengthened my belief that I was going to win, but little by little he got back into it.

It was a rainy Sunday afternoon and we only played five games before they abandoned play for the day, which created the first Monday final ever. When I won the first set having been 0-3 down and restarting at 2-3, I felt overconfident. Usually you don't, you have to stay humble, but I had a good record against Edberg, I'd won the title in 1985 and '86, and I felt it was natural that I would win this thing again. As a result I was caught totally by surprise on the Monday. My mentality was weak and wrong, and he took advantage, pure and simple. The tiebreak in the second set was the turning point, and by the end he was taking me apart. It was 6-2 in the fourth, and I was beside myself.

Left: **I check the net after serving a double-fault at Wimbledon in 1988.**

I thought that was my title, and it wasn't. It was a sort of wake-up call, and given what was happening in the background, 'wake-up call' is a very appropriate expression.

Even though I reached four successive Wimbledon finals, and won one of them, the period 1988–90 was marked by an addiction I developed – and subsequently kicked – to sleeping pills.

I started taking sleeping pills to beat jetlag, but I also took them to beat the pressure. You can find all sorts of justifications for taking sleeping pills. I recognised, fairly, that some people sleep better than others. I'm not a great sleeper in general, travelling all year long across five continents makes you tired, and I was struggling to get sleep before some matches. I convinced myself that taking an occasional sleeping pill wasn't a problem – that if I couldn't sleep, I wasn't giving myself the best chance to perform at my best the next day. That may be legitimate, but I was under pressure and was taking the pills partly for that reason rather than just to be an optimum tennis player. I don't think I'm the only athlete to have been hooked on sleeping pills, but I'm one of the very few who admit it.

The pressure I felt under stemmed from losing in the 1987 second round. In the general context it was nothing to be ashamed of, and I was still only 19, but the critics, who were looking for trends before they had even started, were happy to suggest that, even if my claim to fame was more than 15 minutes, it might only be limited to 30 minutes at the most. Although I didn't feel under pressure after losing to Doohan at Wimbledon, the remainder of 1987 went pretty poorly too. After a while I began to feel under pressure again, and I wasn't coping with it. Expectations got to me, starting with myself, and then everywhere I went I felt frustrated. A year earlier I'd been on top of the world – now there were times when I felt I couldn't play tennis any more.

One day, I was with the West German Davis Cup team, and our doctor, the very well-respected Professor Joseph Keul (he was also the German Olympic team doctor), was chatting with us. We were almost joking when we asked him if he had a cure for jetlag. To our surprise, he said it was easy; he had a pill that most athletes take because 'it isn't that strong'. The pill was called Planum, and I don't know where he got the idea that it wasn't that strong – if you took a Planum now, within 15 minutes you wouldn't be able to walk out of the room by yourself – it's that strong. But we believed him, we spent a lot of time in planes, so when you have a 10-hour flight and you have to sleep, it's very tempting to take one, even if it meant that within a quarter of an hour we couldn't make our way to the washroom unaided.

Today I know how wrong and dangerous it is, zooming yourself to sleep like that, but in those days I didn't know and it was so attractive. Yet it drains you. After a couple of difficult nights you get weak and soft. Stupidly, I also took a Planum the night before certain important matches, not realising that the recovery time was much longer than I thought. That's why I was such a slow starter in some matches, and while I don't want to take anything away from Stefan for beating me fair and square in the 1988 Wimbledon final, I think the pills had something to do with it. I wasn't sleeping great on the Friday night, and then again on Saturday night, and then having the final postponed to Monday meant three nights with sleeping pills. That makes your mind weak and makes you unclear about what you want to do the next day, and I think it affected me. The 1988 final was the only match I lost at Wimbledon that was interrupted. Losing in that Wimbledon final taught me a lesson – I became aware of the dangers of sleeping pills, and I cut down on them. But I continued to use them for another three years, and they were partly responsible for another Wimbledon final defeat a couple of years later.

I was determined not to make the same mistake the following year, but I very nearly didn't have a chance to make it to the 1989 final, let alone challenge for it. Fortunately, the rain saved me.

My defeat to Edberg in the 1988 final hardly did me any damage for the rest of the year. I played five more tournaments and two Davis Cup ties, and lost a total of just two matches, and one of those didn't matter as it was a round robin match at the Masters. I won the titles in Cincinnati, Tokyo, Stockholm and the Masters in New York – a title I won on a fifth set tiebreak in the final against Lendl on one of the biggest strokes of luck in my whole career. We had a long baseline rally at 6-5 in the tiebreak, and suddenly I hit a forehand that crashed against the netcord and dropped over stone dead. Two weeks later I achieved one of my life's ambitions: to win the Davis Cup. It was my biggest triumph after Wimbledon, and we'd done it away against a great Sweden team.

***Above:* Patrik Kühnen, Eric Jelen, Carl-Uwe Steeb, captain Niki Pilić and I, after winning the Davis Cup in 1989.**

There's a little story that followed my win on the netcord in New York. It was my first Masters title, I'd lost to Lendl in my other three Masters appearances (1985–87), and I'd finally made it. When I woke up on Monday morning I decided to buy myself something big as a treat. I had befriended an American tennis journalist called Peter Bodo, and he knew Manhattan very well in those days, in particular those parts of the city where tourists don't usually go. He knew which areas were safe and which weren't, how to avoid the drug dealers, and so forth. I loved it because I was intrigued to get to know the real New York.

My plane was leaving on the Monday night and I asked Peter if he could take me to one of the galleries – I didn't know much about art, but I felt I wanted a big painting. He took me to one of the downtown galleries which was selling an Andy Warhol painting. It was of Mick Jagger from three sides – very particular, and very tall. I thought it was great, and I paid $50,000 for it. I brought it back to Europe, but where in Europe? My girlfriend at the time was Karen Schultz, who lived in Hamburg. I was living in Monte Carlo but because of all my travel to tournaments I was seldom there, and I felt it ought to be seen, so I sent the shipment to Karen's apartment in Hamburg where it hung, and I saw it when I went to stay with her. After two or three years unfortunately our relationship ended, and she asked me what I wanted her to do with the painting. I said 'You know what, leave everything. I don't know what to do with it, you seem to like it, I don't know where to put it in Monte Carlo, I'm on the road the whole time anyway. You have it, it's yours.' That was 1991.

After that we kept in touch, we saw each other once a year, Karen wrote me beautiful letters on my birthday and Christmas, and we kept in contact long-distance. She was a really classy girl – my mother and sister both liked her. After studying, she became a school teacher, moved to Dresden, got married, and had a baby daughter. Then in 2009 she contacted me, said unfortunately her marriage hadn't lasted, and that she had to downsize, and the Warhol painting was just too big for her new flat – so could she give it back to me? Karen is a very intelligent and beautiful woman, not financially well off, but she had integrity. I told her she could keep it, but she said no, it didn't feel right for her to have it. The painting was by then worth between €2–3 million! She was struggling financially after the break-up of her marriage, but she said it didn't feel right for her to sell it.

***Left:* Playing a high forehand volley during the West Germany v Sweden Davis Cup final in Stuttgart in December 1989.**

Karen said she would send it to me, but once it was clear that she really didn't want it, I asked my friend and physiotherapist Waldemar Kliesing to drive to her apartment, pick it up, and take it to a safe place. I didn't know where to put it, and at first it went to Leimen where it spent six months in my mother's cellar – I was worried that my mother would spill something on it. Then after six months I decided it wasn't safe and I sent it to a good friend in Munich who's an art expert, and he currently has it until I work out what to do with it. I tell the story to show what a classy person Karen is. It was hers. I kept asking her what I could do for her if she didn't want the painting, but she wouldn't accept anything. She's a different animal, an unbelievable person – they don't make people like her any more.

My good form from the end of 1988 continued into 1989. I won the titles in Milan and Philadelphia, was runner-up in Monte Carlo and had a very good clay season, which meant I went to the French Open full of confidence. I survived a five-setter against Guillermo Perez-Roldan in the fourth round, but those were the only sets I dropped before playing Stefan Edberg in the semis. I knew that waiting in the final was not one of the big names of clay court tennis like Lendl, Wilander or Noah, but a 17-year-old called Michael Chang. It was a golden opportunity for me. I came back from two sets down and was a break up in the fifth, but I lost. I had sleepless nights after that. I can't say I'd have beaten Chang in the final, but I would certainly have been favourite. I felt I'd blown the French.

It made me very motivated for the next Slam, which was Wimbledon, but it also made me feel I had to do something a bit different. So I skipped Queen's and played the tournament in Hoylake, near Liverpool. I won that tournament on the Saturday and played my first match at Wimbledon on the Monday. But it all went well and I felt really strong. I won five matches in straight sets to set up a semi-final against Ivan Lendl.

The one thing that's underestimated by people who haven't played at the highest level is that, because a Grand Slam is two weeks, there's a totally different dynamic about it. You cannot stay on the same emotional level for two weeks, it's impossible, and so you go through ups and downs. Think of any two-week period: how many ups and downs do you go through? That happens to us during a tournament, we are always vulnerable to a low at some stage – therefore some matches we're just pleased to get through, even if the score doesn't look great. I had a low on the day of that semi-final, and because of the French Open loss – also a semi-final – the demons came back, and Lendl took advantage. He was having his best grass court season, he'd won his first title at Queen's with most of the top grass courters in the draw, and he was on a winning streak. I won the first set, but he played a good tiebreaker in the second, and I was so angry about the way I had played the breaker that he broke my serve twice at the start of the third. He had me.

But thankfully the rain came. In those days we didn't have the roof, so with him leading 3-0 on two breaks of serve in the third set, I was pleased to get off court and take a shower. That allowed me to regroup, and then I beat him pretty fair in the fifth set.

That was the break I needed. The semi-final had taken place on Saturday because of rain on the Friday, so I didn't have too much time to think about the final against Edberg. But I was determined not to be careless after the heartache of 1988. I was out for redemption. I was so ready to play because of the pain I'd felt in the previous year that I took the first set 6-0. He got into it in the second, but I beat him in straight sets. It was a great day for West Germany – because of more rain on Saturday, the women's final was played on the Sunday too, and Steffi Graf beat Martina Navratilova, meaning we had two West German winners that day.

***Right:* Because of rain, the men's and women's finals at the 1989 Wimbledon were played on the same day.**

So when people moan about the rain at Wimbledon, I thank my lucky stars for the timing of Saturday's rain. I can honestly say I would have lost to Lendl if the rain hadn't interrupted the match and allowed me to get my senses back. Overall, my level at Wimbledon in 1989 was very close to my level in 1986, which I think of as my best tennis year. But in 1989 it wasn't just my serve that was good – my returns, my volleys, my footwork, and how I approached matches tactically were better than ever before. Yet I still needed that bit of luck on the day I was mentally vulnerable. These are the fine margins that tennis watchers don't always appreciate.

There are a couple of footnotes to Wimbledon 1989 that are worth mentioning. In my second round match against Richard Matuszewski, I was warned for breaking the all-white clothing rule. I've talked about how important it is to me that I am true to myself, and part of my character – at least at that time – was that nobody was going to tell me what to wear. I knew that the clothing rule at Wimbledon was mostly white, but I was suddenly seized by a wish to choose just how white it was going to be. I began the match wearing my white shirt, but in my bag I had a mainly white shirt with a lot of green and blue stripes. In the third set, with the match going very well for me, the devil inside me said 'They're not going to throw me off the court if I'm leading in the third set,' so I put on the striped shirt. And of course afterwards I was asked not to wear that shirt again. That's fine, I got the message; I'd just wanted to test the boundaries. I knew I was doing it, and I accept it now as a reflection of who I was then, even though I've grown up a lot since. Nowadays the same thing wouldn't happen because the top players have their clothing lines that are approved by the club well before Wimbledon begins, so they don't have the shirts in their bag to make the kind of choice I made.

The other footnote concerns my winnings. I never normally picked up my prize money myself, but for some reason in 1989 I did. I was in my tracksuit after the final, I was given the cheque,

so I put it in my pocket – OK, it was for nearly £200,000, but where else was I going to put it? I then forgot all about it, until next day I was asked where the cheque was. I'm not even sure that I knew what a cheque was. We looked for it but couldn't find it; at one stage we feared it had been stolen. We then asked my mother, and she found it in my tracksuit trousers when she was doing my laundry. I remembered that, in the intensity of the time after the final, my mother wanted to be my mother again, and she said 'Son, give me your laundry, I'll do your washing for you.' The problem was she had washed it, so we had to ask Wimbledon for another cheque to present to the bank!

The period from mid-1988 to mid-1991 was my most consistent on all surfaces. It didn't mean I won Wimbledon every year, but I was number one or two in the rankings, first battling with Ivan Lendl, then with Stefan Edberg. And having won my third Wimbledon title, I went on to complete an achievement that was equally special for me.

Wimbledon was always the ultimate prize, but having won it at 17 and 18, I was very keen to show I wasn't just a grass court player. My results on the tour on hard courts, clay and indoor carpet showed that I could play on all surfaces, but I felt I needed to win at least one of the other three Slams to prove myself. I finally made it in September 1989 when I won the US Open. Again, the underestimated nature of surviving seven matches in a fortnight needs to be stressed. On a humid New York day, I was two sets down in the second round against Derrick Rostagno, and two match points down in the fourth set tiebreaker, but I survived. On Rostagno's second match point, I hit a running crosscourt forehand that hit the top of the net and dropped in. That broke his spirit and I ran away with the fifth set, but that's how close I came to losing in the second round of the one US

Left: **My year kept on getting better and better. I celebrate at the US Open 1989.**

Open I managed to win. I dropped sets in the third and fourth rounds, but from then I was OK, and in the final I beat Lendl in four sets to join that rare club of players who have won majors on two different surfaces.

The year finished with West Germany retaining the Davis Cup, this time on home soil against Sweden. It was a great triumph, which featured the second of the three best matches I ever played. I had beaten Edberg on the Friday, but Eric Jelen and I had a marathon doubles on Saturday, which we won 6-4 in the fifth, and with Edberg favourite against Charly Steeb in the fifth, there was a lot of pressure on me to beat Wilander in the first of Sunday's matches to get the third point. I beat him 6-2, 6-0, 6-2, which has to be one of my best performances, not just the tennis but taking into account the importance of the match. And I did it with my friends, so it's different to winning a Grand Slam. But it was perhaps the time when I began to be less German and more international.

It was just five weeks after the Berlin Wall had come down and it was a remarkable time. I was raised as a proud German who had represented the national team, but I was living outside Germany, because I felt more at ease abroad than in Germany. I had the feeling that in Germany people always wanted to pigeonhole me, and I always fought that – there was this internal fight that I didn't want to become what they saw me as.

Suddenly, here was a situation where everyone was rejoicing at the fall of the Berlin Wall and the Iron Curtain. I rejoiced too, but I was less comfortable with everyone saying that the reunification of Germany would be the next step. In a couple of interviews, I said 'Who says? – is reunification really the right thing?' That didn't go down too well back home. And after reunification in October 1990, I did a long interview in which I said that, just because we have reunified with our brothers and sisters, it doesn't mean we're the greatest nation in the world. We have a history, we have to be careful not to repeat it, so

Above: **The effects of sleeping pills really got to me at Wimbledon in 1990.**

we shouldn't get ahead of ourselves; we shouldn't become too arrogant or too powerful. I was basically saying 'Hold on, we've got to stay humble, we've got to keep our feet on the ground'. At a time when everyone was celebrating reunification, I was going against the majority opinion, even though the majority liked me. It probably made me better positioned internationally, but didn't necessarily make me more popular in Germany.

The dreaded sleeping pills had a part to play in the 1990 Wimbledon final that got away. My draw was moderately tough, as I came up against Pat Cash again, this time in the fourth round. It was very early for two title contenders to meet. It was partly due to the fact that we only had 16 seeds then.

Today's system, in which 32 players are seeded in a draw of 128, was introduced in 2000, the year after I retired as a player. In some ways it's good, but I'm not a fan of it. There are a lot more boring early round matches than there were before. Nowadays the top guys often win 6-1, 6-2, 6-3 up to the middle weekend, which I don't think helps anyone – it's not great for viewers, the ratings aren't great, and there are fewer stories in the first week. Yes, you have two more matches – instead of players having to play five to win the title you have seven, so you can sell more tickets, and you get your marquee names into the latter stages, but quality-wise it's a step down. By contrast, with 16 seeds we'd have a few matches in the first week that were challenging. I'd be happy to cut the majors down to a 64-player draw to make the tournaments shorter.

One thing that hasn't changed since then is that you only have a handful of people who could play on grass, irrespective of the rankings. And Pat was one of them. He claimed to be the best on grass on his best day, certainly grass was always his favourite surface, and he was someone nobody liked to play at Wimbledon. I knew that the majority of the baseliners I played weren't going to beat me, but Pat was a threat. Because of our antipathy from two years earlier, the match was once again hyped, but I beat him in straight sets, and followed it up by beating Brad Gilbert, also in straight sets.

I reached the final by beating Goran Ivanišević in four sets – the third of which by the most unlikely score of 6-0. Goran's biggest demon was always himself, and I'm so happy for him that he actually won Wimbledon at the end of his career. It would not have made sense for a guy with such a natural instinct on grass, with one of the greatest lefty serves of all time, perhaps the greatest, not to have won Wimbledon. In fact it would have been insane, but because of his mental fragility it was possible. And in a tiebreaker I felt I could use a bit of sportsmanship and a bit of cleverness to challenge him mentally. It worked most of the time, and having got back into the match by taking the second set on the tiebreak, I then ran away with the third. For him to lose on grass 6-0 with his serve ought to have been impossible.

The final was different on many levels to 1988, because Stefan was by now a proper competitor for No. 1. We'd had battles, and it was no surprise that we were both in the final. I knew from the start that this was going to be a 50:50 match, whereas in 1988 I was a clear-cut favourite. I had another slow start. I don't remember when I took the last sleeping pill, but it was already light outside, and I really struggled to get to the courts on time – I feel the need to apologise to the spectators watching, it was crazy. So it was no surprise that I went 6-2, 6-2 down, but I felt the longer the match went the better I got. I got back to two sets all, and I was up 3-1 in the fifth set. I don't think I had ever lost a match when I was a break up in the fifth set. But I did that day.

I was serving at 3-1, and I missed a forehand volley at 30-15. I missed it because I had a soft hand. I went back to the baseline after that point, and I thought 'Hmm, I'm nervous now.' I wasn't used to that, I was seldom nervous, but I was then, perhaps for the

***Left:* Slipping at Wimbledon in 1992, not just on the court but in life, as tennis had slipped down my priority list.**

first time in a big final. I wasn't ashamed of it, but I was aware that this was something new. And I went on to lose the final set 6-4.

To lose in a Wimbledon final from being a break up in the fifth set, to be so close to winning my fourth Wimbledon, was heartbreaking, but I need to say something about losing. The longer you play tennis the more you understand that winning and losing go together. It isn't a one-way street where you win all the time – you have players who lose a lot more than they win, but they still have to be respected. When you're younger, innocence helps you – the fact that you feel unbeatable, the strongest kid in town, means you just don't think of losing, but the older you get the more matches you play and you lose more, and you understand that it's part of the package. The 1990 Wimbledon final, tough though it was, didn't destroy me. Going into the match I knew it was going to be a battle, and on the day I lost. You should always be competitive, but you should never get too down with losing or too high with winning, because the margin between them can be very small.

Those who remember me at Wimbledon in 1991 probably remember a tortured soul. People say I could barely string a coherent sentence together, and if they remember that, they have good reason. I was an emotional wreck by then. I was confused; I was losing my mind. To work out the reasons why, you have to go back 18 months to the start of 1990.

By the end of 1989 I was already taking stock on my career. I'd won a third Wimbledon title, I'd won my first US Open, and we'd defended our Davis Cup title. One thing I had never done, however, was to finish a year as No. 1, so I decided in the new year to really go for it. I entered lots of tournaments, but I had what seemed like a shadow: Stefan Edberg. The guy read me! He entered the same tournaments, I won three finals out of four against him, but he was still ahead of me in the rankings. The fourth of those finals was in Paris Bercy, one of the last tournaments of the year. I was struggling more than him physically, I pulled a thigh muscle at 3-3 in the first set and had to retire. He therefore went to the ATP World Championship (the old Masters which that year had moved from Madison Square Garden in New York to the Festhalle (festival hall) in Frankfurt), ranked No. 1, with me at No. 2.

After the Paris final I phoned my trusted doctor Hans-Wilhelm Müller Wohlfahrt in Munich, and asked him what I had to do to be ready for Frankfurt eight days later. The guy said 'Listen Boris, you can't play.' I told him that wasn't an option for me, I had spent the whole year aiming to finish No. 1, and I wasn't going to refuse to jump the last fence – I had to play. He heard me and said he'd do his best, but he said I couldn't practise, as he had to do four treatments, one every second day. The treatment took eight days, and I couldn't play tennis during the treatment. I flew from Paris to Munich on the Sunday night for the first treatment. He then flew with me to Frankfurt, the last treatment was on the Monday, my first match was on the Tuesday, and I went into it without hitting a tennis ball since Bercy.

By some miracle I won my round robin matches, including beating Lendl in the last of them to send him packing. But Stefan won all his matches too. So you had a semi-final line-up of Edberg playing Sampras, followed by me against Agassi. The problem was that if Edberg beat Sampras, he'd be guaranteed the year-end No. 1 ranking. And he did, at which point my motivation disappeared, and Agassi crushed me.

At that point I did something I'd never done before – I skipped a press conference, for which I was fined around $1,000, and decided to walk back to my hotel. This was the middle of November, it was pouring with rain, and I was still in my shorts and tracksuit top. There was an official courtesy car, but I'd told the driver not to pick me up. So he drove just behind me while I walked, utterly frustrated, back to the hotel.

Right: **The 1990 final - I was a break up in the final set but got nervous and lost to Edberg.**

FILA
FILA

It was like a scene from some *film noir*. You couldn't talk to me, I was in too much pain.

When the frustration subsided, all I could think of was 'When can I catch him, when can I catch him? What do I have to do? I have to play again.' That left me without the desire to have a holiday, so I worked through the off-season. But it backfired on me. With the first tournament of 1991 taking place in Adelaide, I went to Australia in early December to get used to the heat and prepare for 1991. I lost in the first round in Adelaide to Magnus Larson, 7-6 in the final set.

I was mentally finished. I said I couldn't take any more, it was too much of a burden, and I seriously considered not playing the Australian Open. It was still another three weeks away, and it was so goddamn hot in Adelaide, 42 and 43°C in the shade, that I just couldn't handle it. Bob Brett was still my coach, and he said 'Look, you're here now, why don't you just give it a try? You're in Melbourne now where it's sunny, back home it's snowy and rainy.' So I decided to stay, but without any great conviction.

Then in the third round of the Australian Open I played an Italian, Omar Camporese, and beat him in well over five hours, 14-12 in the fifth. That's when I was tested. I was the favourite, but throughout the match I was on an emotional roller coaster. The match was played on an outside court; we started at three, and finished about nine. It was the longest match at the Australian Open until recently, at five hours and 11 minutes. At the end I felt I'd gone through hell – but I had come through it, and I was ready now. I went on to win the Australian Open and, just as importantly, become No. 1 in the rankings for the first time.

For me that was the end of a long journey. All the anguish that had started with losing to Edberg in the Wimbledon final six months earlier, that had continued with my failure to catch him as the year-end No. 1, and the manic start to the year that almost came to a crushing halt in Adelaide – I had come through it all and achieved my aim of seeing my name at the top of the rankings. I'd like to have had the perspective I have now, to have smiled sweetly and accepted the congratulations, but I was already at the edge of my emotions.

Left: In 1991 I was in such emotional turmoil that I don't think I made much sense.

I bounced around with delight after shaking Lendl's and the umpire's hand at the end of the match, but then I ran out of the stadium. I didn't want to be part of the ceremony. I said to myself, 'This is my win, I don't want to celebrate it with anyone', and I ran to the hotel. One of the ground officials followed and talked some sense into me. He told me the whole world was watching and I had to come back to accept the trophy. But I was so wild, I told him 'I've put so much effort into this, all the struggling in November and December, this moment is just for me.' I did go back eventually, but there was a quarter-of-an-hour delay because I had run away. And I had run away, literally and metaphorically.

Getting to No. 1 and being able to say that I was the best in the world in my profession wasn't an easy thing to handle. I said at the time that I couldn't see myself staying there for five years, and I think from that point I started to think of different aspects of my life. In retrospect, from that moment tennis was no longer everything for me, but it took my Wimbledon experience six months later for me to really grasp the message.

So a lot had happened by the time I got to Wimbledon in June 1991, nearly a year after my defeat to Edberg. I was so tired and drained after Australia and didn't play many tournaments, and the thigh injury came back to cut the middle out of my clay season. I did reasonably well, including reaching another semi-final at the French Open – people forget that and don't give me credit for it. I'd lost the No. 1 ranking during the clay season, but I was within striking distance of regaining it. And when Michael Stich beat Edberg in four sets in the semi-finals and I beat David Wheaton, I knew I'd be No. 1, whether or not I won the final.

It all looked so good to the world. I was in the final, back at No. 1, and I had Katarina Witt in my box, which the German media loved because the golden girl of East Germany and the golden boy of West Germany were together (even though she was only ever a close friend, never a girlfriend). But emotionally I was a mess.

I had made up my mind before Wimbledon began that if I won the title, I would retire. And I meant it – or I would have definitely had a long break at the very least. I went into the final against Michael Stich knowing that if I won it, it would be my last match. That was a foolish thing to do, but it tells you where I was emotionally. I was tired of the whole thing, the whole machinery of tennis – the rankings, the travelling, everything. And as a result the final was a very frustrating match. I don't think I've ever behaved so badly in a match as in that final. I think it was just my inner voice. I can't watch the highlights now I was so miserable. And I lost in straight sets.

After the match, I remember going back to my rented house in Wimbledon with a sense of relief. And I just started crying. I'd never cried before, but I was in tears for a long time. I'm not the crying type, but I was venting my relief that I didn't have to make the decision to retire which I'd promised myself I'd do if I won the final. So I felt good on the Monday morning that my journey would continue, but obviously the motivation went. I knew I had to look for something else besides tennis, because the game wasn't giving me enough substance and satisfaction. I knew how to play it, I'd been doing it for a long time, I'd made some money, I'd been Wimbledon champion and I'd been No. 1, but what was the next motivation? The answer came to me then: I said 'I have to get my private life in order.'

I realised that, in order for me to get back to the top and take it as seriously as I needed to, I just had to create a more balanced private life, which in effect meant I was looking for a wife. I needed a life away from tennis because tennis was killing me. That's what made my idol Björn Borg stop at 25. Borg had no life outside tennis, and when you're as emotionally wrapped up as we were, you need that. McEnroe, Sampras and Edberg were different; they never got as emotionally wrapped up as I did. Agassi was a bit like me; he needed his private life to be in balance to play well. At that point in July 1991, I felt my private life was more important than my professional life. I was very confused: the only thing I had was tennis; outside tennis I was troubled, and I didn't have an exit strategy. I was only 24, and I knew what had happened to Borg – I didn't want to stop, but I needed a reason to find the time to work at it.

My defeat to Michael in the Wimbledon final of 1991 was a tough loss. I would love to have won a fourth Wimbledon title, but I benefited from the loss more than if I'd have won. And yet if you play by the umpire's call, I did win Wimbledon. John Bryson, who was in the chair for that final, made a mistake. When Michael won the winning point, Bryson said 'Game Set and Match Becker', and it was only after all the handshakes that he corrected himself and said 'Game Set and Match Stich'. Given how much was riding on it for me, what an irony there was in that misspoken line! Two months later I met Barbara.

Right: **I broke plenty of eggs with my serve...**

FILA

1991

What else was going on in the world in 1991, the year I reached the top of the rankings? There was a lot happening, and it coincided with my emergence as someone genuinely interested in the wider world.

Those were days when everything was a bit fragile and I was becoming aware of life around me, of politics, of greater things than winning and losing a tennis match. That made it more difficult to find the motivation to play. I wanted to know more, so it was tempting to read more and practise less. It also meant I just couldn't take a quarter-final in Indianapolis that seriously if something major had happened in the world the previous day.

We tennis players live in a very small bubble, and we can be extremely earnest athletes at times. Some players are completely oblivious to the outside world, but I couldn't be (and Novak is like that today). It may mean we lack the tunnel vision to win a Slam final on a certain day, but the other side of the coin is that we are human beings and citizens of the world with an open mind. To some people I became the thinking man's player, the intellectual, and the socialist. I was none of these – I was just a young man growing up and questioning everything a bit, and that's something that at 25 you should do.

I don't want to claim that any of the turbulent events affected me directly, but the USA sending troops and Scud missiles into Kuwait for 'Operation Desert Storm' happened during the Australian Open. They were there to drive out Iraqi forces who had occupied the country in late 1990, and I remember it as the first television war. I flew back over that region from Australia, and for the first time I was aware that life wasn't as safe as I'd believed up to then. I was very moved by it, it put my search for No. 1 into a perspective – it makes you enjoy your life more when you compare your own lot to that of others who are a lot less fortunate.

Although I hadn't yet met Barbara, I remember vividly being shocked by the story of Rodney King, a black citizen of Los Angeles who was brutally beaten by white police officers, leading to rioting in Los Angeles over how the police appeared to view blacks differently to whites. I always had a sensitive spot for African-Americans. I loved their music, their style, their behaviour, and I have many friends who are black sporting stars, like Yannick Noah – so any discrimination against blacks was always big for me.

It seems odd but Germany was finally given full independence following the Second World War after the occupying powers agreed to give up all remaining rights. During the period 1989–91 that included the fall of the Berlin Wall, the reunification of Germany and then full independence, I spent a lot of time with my girlfriend Karen Schultz who lived in Hamburg, not far from the East German border. Her family were from the East, and we went through Checkpoint Charlie many times, so I had a good understanding of what this was about.

Lech Walesa was elected president of Poland, ending a decade-long struggle for the Solidarity trade union. I was very interested in this movement, even though it was a socialist party, albeit a democratic one. Why would someone in my world – where you have all the capitalists, the conservatives, the rich and famous – take an interest in this? It was a question I could never answer, and still can't. I do vote – I believe if you don't vote, you aren't entitled to an opinion and should shut up. I've voted for conservatives and social-democrats, I'm a believer today in Angela Merkel, but on some points I'm alternative or Green. Your mindset changes when you run your own company, you become more conservative.

Among the other things that happened that year, I remember the picture of Niki Lauda on the site of the wreckage of the Lauda Air Boeing 767 that crashed near Bangkok. Niki Lauda is a friend of mine and I've followed his career from world champion to successful businessman. Mike Tyson was arrested and charged with raping Miss Black America in Indianapolis – I had been in the same hotel a month earlier, I was there for the tournament, and that's why I remember the story.

Chapter 6

Still a factor (1992–96)

'Far more important than any tennis match.'

I cried with relief all night in my rented house in Wimbledon on the night of the lost final of 1991. I never normally do that, but it was a sign of how much emotional tension had built up. Now I had the outcome I wanted – I could go on playing, but I knew tennis was not everything in my life

The first recognition in tennis was that I decided my ranking was comfortable for the rest of the year. You keep your ranking points for a full year, and having won the Australian Open, been runner-up at Wimbledon and semi-finalist at the French Open, I was going to stay in the top five. But I was no longer challenging for No. 1, because I'd done it already, and the year-end No. 1 no longer interested me because I couldn't muster the necessary energy, time and motivation. After all, I was already insane in July, so there was no way I could sustain that to the end of the year.

It meant I cherry picked my tournaments. I played few matches – more or less when I wanted to play and when I felt good about playing. It meant I lost some early matches, including at the US Open. The ATP World Championships were always important to me, and I qualified, but I failed to make it through the round-robin stage. But what the results websites don't show was that I met my wife in September, and after everything I had gone through up to and including Wimbledon, that was much more important to me than any tennis tournament.

We met by accident in a restaurant. I was dining in Munich with a group of people, one of whom was Sophie Ţiriac, the ex-wife of Ion Ţiriac. Sophie's best friend was Barbara Feltus, a model whose mother was white and her father was black – in other words, she was mixed race, but to most Germans she was black. Since Sophie knew Barbara liked me, she invited her to join us. I was instantly attracted to her, and shortly afterwards we became an item.

In those days it had become more important who I had dinner with rather than which tournament I'd won, as the gossip would sell more newspapers. And against that background, it was a massive story when I – one of Germany's sporting heroes and a very typical German-looking white guy – began dating a black girl.

The story of my relationship with Barbara deserves a doctoral thesis of its own, just for the mirror it held up to Germany's view of people with a different skin colour. I didn't mind it being serious headline news, but there was a nasty overtone to a lot of it. I was portrayed as the rebel. People made a variety of comments, essentially saying 'How could I date a black girl?' I wasn't going to apologise for it – I loved this woman, and she was a fully-fledged German. She was born in Heidelberg to a German mother and had grown up in Germany; she can even speak in Heidelberg dialect when the mood takes her. OK, so her father was a black American, but so what? Yet that was enough to make many people feel she wasn't German, and I felt that was wrong. Eventually, I provoked reactions by agreeing to

Right: **My relationship with Barbara was always of interest to the media.**

FILA
FABER

go on the cover of *Stern* magazine with both of us naked. I was standing behind Barbara covering her breasts with my arm in a warm embrace; there was nothing indecent about it, but the point the photo made was the black and white skin. In the article that accompanied the photo, I spoke about racism and us both having the same problems in life, to make the point that getting fixated on skin colour was just silly.

Looking back, I hope I helped the German people to reach an understanding of how having a different skin colour is not as big an obstacle as they thought. In the early 1990s, as now, there were many women in Germany with differing skin colours, but they weren't called German, they were given names like 'mixed race', 'black' and so forth. So maybe that was an eye-opener to some people in Germany: that you can have some genuine Germans who don't fit the look that most Germans expect a typical German to have. And I hope I helped them towards that understanding. Things have changed a little, especially with the number of players of Turkish origin in the German national football team, but even now there are still many people who have difficulty accepting that you can be German and not have white skin.

Perhaps not surprisingly, mixed-race Germans became my biggest supporters, and that's the case to this day. Although Barbara and I have now been divorced for longer than we were married, I still have my mixed-race boys, and I live my whole life with people of different ethnic backgrounds, and mixed-race people respond positively to that. If you like, it's a political view without trying to be political, which makes it more credible because I'm actually living it.

Partly because of my relationship with Barbara and partly because of other statements and comments I'd made, I started to become less a sportsman and more of a personality who is famous for tennis, but who also has opinions about the world of politics and social issues. I had always read about the world and taken an interest in it, but I felt I was never asked about my opinions in the locker room, or by the media. I wanted to make Germany look at itself: the natural German approach is to follow orders, and I felt people should think more. There was some rebelliousness in there, but also a principle.

Left: Being born in November meant I often ended the year on my birthday, and in 1992 I won the ATP World Championship in Frankfurt on the day.

As I've said, there was a lot going on in 1991 – I was concerned about the Iraq-Kuwait war at the start of the year, we had the attempted coup against the Soviet leader Mikhail Gorbachev in the summer, and it was the first year after the reunification of Germany. I felt I could say things because I'd been to Africa, to Australia, to America, and most Germans hadn't. And since I'm supposed to be a German role model I might as well talk about what I'd seen with my German eyes. I felt I could legitimately talk about such things, it wasn't as boring as forehands or backhands, and I think the resonance was good. Looking back, it probably put me on a higher platform; I wasn't just considered a good tennis player but probably the most international German in those days. It didn't mean I knew everything about politics, of course, but I had an opinion to which I was entitled, and I talked about it. That pleased me, and it gave me a new zest for life, a new comfort zone, and it helped to prolong my tennis career.

It would be wrong to think I just had opinions that came from nowhere. I was doing a lot of reading at that time. I was into Hermann Hesse's *Siddhartha*, and other books that amounted to heavy intellectual stuff for somebody 'just' playing tennis. I felt there was a void – that there was something I wanted to know and needed to learn; I wanted to understand other high-profile people's lives, what they went through, maybe in the hope that I could pick up something. I became crazy about biographies – from Michael Jordan to Marlon Brando. I loved the one about Brando, I felt very close to his life and what he went through.

I was also fond of the biography of Muhammad Ali, *The Fight* by Norman Mailer, which became my ritual reading before matches – I read it all the time because it gave me so much to think about. I read them all – you name one, I've probably read it. That was my theme. They filled the void; they gave me something no-one could tell me. We're talking about the days before the internet, and in those days more people read books. I became a *thinking* tennis player, almost an intellectual tennis player. I said we could talk about tennis, but let's also talk about the communist party, or about the Cold War, or about racism – I was more interested in talking and learning about those subjects rather than my tennis-playing form. I felt good about that, I felt satisfied.

I also felt I had a bit of catching up to do with the press. I knew that in some of my press conferences in the period up to Wimbledon 1991 I was probably giving the wrong impression due to the state I was in. I didn't like that and at times I wanted to explain why I seemed a difficult character – why I didn't speak much or why I seemed reclusive. I was reclusive because I needed to find a bit of strength – and I accepted that the press had to write about that, but I wanted to give an explanation about why I was like that, and that the real Boris Becker was much more interested in world affairs than just about tennis.

If you look at my results over the three years from Wimbledon 1991, you could view my career as being in a bit of a lull. I think of the lull as being only about 18 months. I believe that all top-level athletes have one lean or 'dog year' in every seven – so if you count back to my first Wimbledon, I could be forgiven for having a 'dog year' from the second half of 1991. But there were plenty of highlights in the lull.

Having reached six finals in seven years at Wimbledon, most people saw my defeat in the 1992 quarter-finals as a disappointment. Yes, it was disappointing, but I lost to Andre Agassi in five sets and most guys would love to be in the Wimbledon quarter-finals just once, so I didn't disrespect myself. Agassi, meanwhile, seemed to be charmed at Wimbledon that year – he went on to win the title, beating Goran Ivanišević in the final. I'd also won two five-setters that year, one against Martin Damm in the second round when I didn't play well, the other against Wayne Ferreira. Wayne and I were locked at two-sets-all on Monday night, and I won the fifth set on Tuesday before playing Agassi on Wednesday. My ability to win interrupted matches at Wimbledon was still alive and well.

One of the biggest highlights of my career came in the middle of 1992 at the Barcelona Olympics, but it was a strange one. I went to the Olympics as a member of the German team. I stayed in the Olympic village in the German apartment. I lost early in singles, but I was still in the doubles, and my doubles partner had also lost early in the singles, so we could both focus on the doubles. The only problem was that we couldn't stand each other. My partner was, of course, Michael Stich.

I've talked already about my relationship with Michael – about how we didn't hate each other and that we were simply not friends. But the rivalry both as top-level tennis players and as German sportsmen meant there were times when relations between us were really not good, and one such time was in Barcelona. We were ranked pretty much the same, both in the top five, he'd beaten me in the Wimbledon final in 1991, and we weren't speaking to each other. I was partly at fault, because I saw him as a competitor who could beat me and I didn't want to give anything away. Up to the quarter-finals we literally would meet an hour before the match, warm up a little together in silence, and then play and win. We had a walkover in the first round so we didn't have to talk to each other, and then we beat the Greeks, Tasos Bavelas and Constantinos Efremoglou, which we could also do without speaking.

That set up a quarter-final against Sergio Casal and Emilio Sanchez. They were one of the best pairs of their era, they were

in form having won a clay court tournament in Austria the week before, and they were both Catalans so they were red-hot home favourites. It was then that Niki Pilić, who was the German men's tennis captain at the Olympics, got Michael and me round a table and said, 'Guys, for you to beat Casal and Sanchez, you have to speak, you have to communicate – otherwise you're going to lose.' So we started talking, we developed some sort of chemistry, and we ended up winning in five sets. We even hugged each other at the end. After months of not talking to each other, a great friendship suddenly blossomed – or at least a friendship for the weekend. We had another five-setter in the semis against Frana and Christian Miniussi of Argentina, but we came through it. We beat the South Africans Ferreira and Piet Norval in the final in four sets. In those few days we spoke at lunch, we acted like we were normal, and we ended up winning the gold medal!

Above: **Michael Stich and I won gold in Barcelona just days after barely being on speaking terms with each other.**

Afterwards, I organised a big dinner with all the German team who were still in Barcelona, but Michael wasn't there. He left the locker room after the medal ceremony and went straight to the airport with his tracksuit on. The friendship for the weekend was over. I later learned that his wife had told him to head straight to the airport, but I didn't know that at the time and I was very upset. That was the last time we spoke for months, and even today I've never celebrated the gold medal with him. I'd like to. I won it because of him, and he won it because of me, but we still haven't celebrated it properly. Maybe for the 25th anniversary in 2017 we can do it? We've laughed about it, but we still haven't done it.

As I've said, we were rivals, so up to a point it was understandable that there were tensions between us, but we took it too far. Why? I think we're very different people. By nature I'm a bit more emotional than he is. I'm more family oriented, I have kids, I like my friends and family with me, I like to hug people, I'm a hugger by nature whereas I don't think he's a natural hugger. There's a stereotypical contrast between the northern and southern Germans that says the northerners are stiffer and more organised, while the southerners are more happy-go-lucky and free-and-easy. Too much is made of it, but in many ways he's a typical northerner from Hamburg while I'm a typical southerner from Baden. So by nature our characters are different. Neither of us meant anything bad by it, we were just raised that way, but it backfired on our relationship.

I always felt that when we were teammates, we were genuine teammates. We could hug each other and give each other high fives, and we could mean it, but what held us together was no more than the need to be united for the sake of the team. You've got to want it on both sides, and when we wanted it, we could unite for the cause. We played a year of Davis Cup tennis together in 1995, and we very nearly got to the final, but in truth we were trying to do the best we could. I put my hands on his shoulders to console him when he lost the fifth set of the fifth match in our semi-final, because it was heartbreaking for him and for all of us in the team, but no-one could think we were anything other than team colleagues.

My tennis began to look up at the end of 1992. For most of the year I'd spent more time building up my private life, my love for my wife, and thinking about a family – I very quickly felt it was the right time to start a family with Barbara because I loved her. That took away the focus of playing better tennis, which I was perfectly happy with. I gave myself the time to keep both my playing career ticking over while focusing more on my relationship; I was still good enough to be in the top 10, but not challenging higher. And as I got the balance right, I started to play good tennis again.

Having Barbara made travelling and practising easier, because I knew there was a 'before' and 'after'. Prior to meeting her, it was just practising and travelling, and it didn't matter whether I was in London, Melbourne or Munich, but now there was something to look forward to after matches and in off-weeks. I also had a new coach, Günter Bresnik. Bresnik is an Austrian who puts a lot of emphasis on the physical side, and I was ready for that, I needed to be fitter. I finished the year strongly, including winning the ATP World Championship in Frankfurt, beating the world No. 1 Jim Courier in straight sets in the final. That meant I was back in the top five. So I went into 1993 with a lot of optimism.

I also had another haircut at the start of 1993. I went for a very short crew cut, and with my closely cropped beard I probably gave the impression of being some Parisian intellectual from the left bank of the Seine. I firmly believe your look is an expression of your soul and I guess that's how I felt. I didn't really care about materialistic, external things – I felt that, especially in my world, the importance of material things was too high. The sporting world is more about individuals and money than about building character, but character was important to me and I wanted to express that.

People look back on 1993 and think it wasn't a great year for me, but I think they overlook two things. One was that my focus was on my private life; the other was the emergence of Pete Sampras. Pete had broken onto the scene when he won the US Open at 19 in 1990. That was almost too early for him, and he struggled with the pressure for the next year or two. But by the middle of 1993 he was ready to take the tennis world by storm, and I was unfortunate enough to be in his path.

The 1993 Wimbledon Championship was a strange one. In those years I knew clay would be harder and harder for me, so

Right: **By the 1992 US Open I was more relaxed again.**

FILA

I focused more on the surfaces that would suit my game, which were grass and indoors, and that meant basing my year around Wimbledon. I thus came to Wimbledon feeling good about how I was playing on grass. In those days, I always did a pre-Wimbledon chat with the German media, it felt the right thing to do. All they were interested in was my first round match. I had been drawn against Marc-Kevin Goellner, a nice guy who had grown up in various places around the world since his German parents had been in the diplomatic service. He'd had a big breakthrough in the clay tournaments, and as I wasn't playing Davis Cup that year, he was the No. 2 singles player behind Michael Stich in the German team. Chatting to the press made me realise it was a big deal in Germany, whereas to me playing Goellner on grass felt like a good draw. It shows that the level of performance I still had was underestimated, and that the German media were getting ahead of themselves about who they thought would be Germany's next big player. So I smiled a little, and beat him fairly easily.

Above: **By Wimbledon 1993 I knew I was going to become a dad, even though the world didn't.**

My big match that year was playing Stich in the quarter-finals. It was a rematch of the 1991 final and he had developed since then into a very good all-round player. In fact 1993 was his best – he finished the year ranked second behind Sampras, and he won the Davis Cup pretty much single-handed. At that time, he was probably better than me overall, but at Wimbledon I liked my chances, and it felt like a final for me. I beat him in five sets in a match that finished in near-darkness, and it felt like a sort of redemption.

The conclusion of the Stich match made the semi-finals so much harder because physically I was struggling. I had a day off, of course, but even with Bresnik's fitness work I was not in the greatest shape in those days, I felt Sampras was going to be tough, and he was. He beat me in three tight sets. I was obviously in good form, but I didn't really have a chance. Afterwards I was trying to explain to people just how good Sampras was, in fact as good as they come on grass. There were echoes of the time I had beaten Johan Kriek in the Queen's final of 1985. Then the media felt Kriek was trying to explain away a bad defeat against me by saying I might win Wimbledon, when what he was saying was that I was better than they thought. This time the media said I was just praising Pete because I'd lost and wanted it to look better, but I asked them to trust their eyes – they'd seen the match, I couldn't touch his serve for three sets, and my return wasn't bad. Again you need your best perspective – facing Sampras in a semi-final wasn't bad. Today everyone agrees with that, but in those days only the player on the other side of the net can tell how good the opposition is, and I was one of the first people to spot that. I had no regrets, I wasn't whining, I just lost to the better guy. I'd beaten Stich in a very good match and I'd done as well as I could, so it made the departure from Wimbledon and the remainder of the year easier.

The happiest day of my life – up to that point – came in the summer of 1993. We found out that Barbara was pregnant. Getting past the third month was also a bit of a relief, because I had the German tennis press on my back, wanting to know why my form wasn't good. I was still fifth or seventh in the rankings, but they'd been used to me being a regular in the top four, and it hadn't worked out with Günter Bresnik. Thus, just before the US Open, I sat down with the German media and said, 'Let me tell you my friends, I'm delighted to announce that my girlfriend and wife-to-be is pregnant with my first child, so that is far more important than any tennis match, and now you know the reason why my form isn't what it was a couple of years ago.' They all clapped and finally understood why I was in this limbo.

I wasn't going to miss the birth of my first child, so with the baby due in late January, I skipped the Australian Open. The morning Noah was born, I was shuffling between the delivery room and a lounge next door with a television which was showing the Australian Open night session. Due to the delivery taking a couple of hours, I was going back and forth, watching the match between Michael Stich and MaliVai Washington. I remember saying to myself, 'My brother has to win this match for me'. By 'my brother' I didn't mean Michael, my brother was MaliVai, because I felt very close to the race. It was not against Michael, I didn't want him to lose, but after all the angst and anguish Barbara and I had gone through in the previous two years with racially motivated comments, I really felt that supporting the black guy was supporting 'my brother'. And he did win.

A few hours later, my son Noah was born. Apart from the joy of becoming a father, I felt my tormented soul had been laid to rest with Noah's birth. Everything felt right – I was a father, I felt refreshed and rejuvenated, and even the result of the Stich-Washington match had gone the right way. I was still young, I was only 26, but when you've won your first Slam at 17, those first 10 years are really long. Noah's birth gave me a kick-start about re-engaging with my first love: playing tennis. I remember going out to the courts the next day and I practised more than I'd practised in a while, and I was able to sustain that level. With my private life going well, and my hunger for tennis back, I felt 1994 would be a lot better.

And it would need to be. Within a few days of Noah's birth, Sampras had won the Australian Open, which meant he had won the last three Grand Slam titles and was the runaway world No. 1, with Agassi, Stich, Courier and Ivanišević his closest challengers. I had a lot of ground to make up.

There was a little incident in my third round match at Wimbledon in 1994 that leads me on to what I see as a big problem in today's tennis.

I was playing Javier Frana on No. 1 Court, and after one set I asked to go to the bathroom and have a bit of treatment on my back. I felt that my back was blocked a little bit, and I wanted my physio to unblock it. If I hadn't needed the bathroom, I could have been treated on court, but I went to the locker room, and my physio treated my back quickly. He did it in front of everybody, on the floor next to the toilet – there was nothing secret about it, and a line umpire was there watching me. I didn't know I wasn't supposed to do that. I wasn't aware of all the rules, so I was fined. If it had been an ATP trainer, that would have been OK, but the fact that it was my own personal trainer treating me in the locker room meant I was fined .

I have no complaints about the fine – I didn't know the rules well enough, I'd broken them, so it's right that I should have some punishment. But I wasn't trying to steal an advantage. At that time, the rules were written so that if you had an injury, you could have it treated, but if you were simply in less good condition than your opponent, then the rules wouldn't save you. They do now.

Under today's rules, if someone is tired or feels like he's about to start cramping, he can take a timeout and get treated. To me, that is wrong. It also doesn't look good, because nobody sees the injury. A big part of trying to win a long match is to try and outlast your opponent, perhaps by making him tired so you can play better in the fourth and fifth sets. That element is totally taken away if the opponent can say 'I think my leg is hurting' even though you see nothing. He then takes a timeout that takes away his opponent's momentum – they can cool down, recharge their batteries, and it's almost like the match starts again. That's totally against the whole concept of one against one, and I get furious as both a commentator and a coach if one guy has the other on the ropes and then the one on the ropes can simply take a timeout. That's just wrong.

I'm not saying there should be no treatment mid-match, and of course I don't want anyone to make an injury worse by playing on when they should stop or have some strapping. If someone twists an ankle or falls down and is in pain, then yes, get a doctor out there. But if you're not injured, if your shoulders are just a bit tight, you shouldn't get any treatment. People will say I'm encouraging those who have cramp or who are on the ropes to act as if they have an injury – well if someone can act so well that they look injured when they're not, then I'm happy to give them the benefit of the doubt. But umpires should be given the chance to make a judgement and either say, 'You're clearly injured, I'll call the trainer for you' or 'I see no injury, play on'.

Of course you get borderline cases. Take the 2014 Australian Open final, for example. Rafael Nadal had hurt his back in practice; he played the first set apparently with full fitness, but then called the trainer in the second set. The result was that his opponent, Stan Wawrinka, lost his rhythm and Nadal won the third set. As it was a Grand Slam final, you want there to be a contest, you don't want Nadal to withdraw injured and leave the tournament with no final, and I'm not saying he broke any rules. But the rules allowed him to say 'I'm down, I'm not feeling good, let me stop the match.' And that cannot be good for the integrity of tennis.

If today's rules were applied in my day, you can be sure we'd have made maximum use of them. You can guarantee that with McEnroe, Connors, Lendl, myself and 25 others, when we were down a set and a break we'd have definitely called a timeout and got the doctor to treat us for 10 minutes. I'm not in favour of going back to the rules in my playing days. They changed the rules because of one high-profile case of cramping where

***Right:* By 1994 I was a father, and my form had really picked up.**

lotto
lotto

the player was in agony and couldn't get any help, and I accept that didn't look good. So the rules shouldn't be quite as strict as they were in my day – if a player is seriously cramping or having a serious injury, then of course they should have treatment. But it's a very soft rule that can be used – and is being abused – to break the opponent's rhythm. I think it is an incorrect rule change that should be partially reversed.

I lost to Goran Ivanišević in the semi-finals that year (1994). On the one hand it was a bad match on my part, and it was the first time I lost at Wimbledon to someone who didn't go on to win the title (other than the Doohan and Scanlon matches). But on the other hand it was also the first time I was seriously challenging for the title again. That was my attitude as I left Wimbledon, so while I wasn't satisfied, I felt my chances of beating him had been good, and I came off court upset rather than seriously disappointed. In fact it relit my fire – I realised I didn't like losing like that, and it made me want to get back to the practice court and work even harder, because I thought I was better than him.

The results were good. I got in shape, I won Basel and Stockholm and I was again competing at the highest level. In Stockholm, a tournament where I always did well, I beat the top three players in the world in successive days (Stich, Sampras and Ivanišević), and I made it to the final of the ATP World Championships where I lost to Sampras in four sets. I felt I was back: I'd had a baby, I'd got back to a high level, and I was eager to practise a bit more.

Just how well I was playing in 1995 was shown more on clay than on grass. I had never won a clay court title, and there I was in April with two match points to win the prestigious Monte Carlo Open. I was up against Thomas Muster in the final. To get to match point against Muster that year was quite something, but the way the match was won and lost had a drama all of its own, and it made headlines for all the wrong reasons.

Muster was on an amazing unbeaten streak on clay, and he went on to win the French Open, his only Grand Slam title. But I was in good shape to challenge on clay again. Muster had a long semi-final on the Saturday against his stable mate Andrea Gaudenzi – he won it 7-6 in the third, and then had to go to hospital for dehydration with the final against me the following day. Two hours before the final was due to start, I was told by the tournament director that Muster wouldn't show up, but I had to wait until 2pm before I was crowned the champion. Knowing Muster for a long time, I knew that until he shook my hand I wouldn't believe him.

An hour before the match, he walked into the locker room and started warming up. I couldn't believe my eyes. In a way I didn't want to win a final without playing, but then again having never won a final on clay I would have gladly accepted it. The final was best-of-five – that was the norm in tour finals back then – and I won the first two sets. But it was a hot day, and the longer we played, the more he played himself into fitness and the more tired I became. I lost the third set, and began thinking 'Hey, wasn't I the winner this morning, shouldn't I be champion by now, and here I am battling against the heat in the fourth set?' But I battled, and we got to the tiebreak. I got to 6-4 – two match points. But then I started cramping. I'd never cramped before. I knew on my serve at 6-4 I had to hit both serves as hard as I could because I couldn't run any more. I missed the first by a tiny margin, and I missed the second by an even tinier margin – it would have been an ace down the middle, but it was a double-fault. He saved the second match point, won the tiebreak, and ran away with the fifth set 6-0.

It was a heartbreaking loss. Yet apart from being as close to winning a clay court title as I ever came, that day became

***Right:* Serving in the emotional Monte Carlo final of 1995 against Thomas Muster.**

FABER

known for something I was supposed to have said afterwards. I was quoted as saying I'd questioned whether Muster was 'clean'. I didn't say that, in fact I didn't say anything in my post-match press conference. What happened is that I muttered something privately while on my way to my press conference. The conference took place on the top floor of the Monte Carlo Country Club building. The locker rooms are at the bottom, so I got into the lift with the official escorting me to the media centre, and as we were chatting, I muttered in bewilderment 'I don't know what they gave him in the hospital.' That was all – I wouldn't be foolish enough to say it at a press conference. But somehow it got out. I don't know how, but the upshot was that I had to make a full retraction. Obviously no athlete is guilty until proven, which is why I didn't say anything publicly. But because that comment got out, I not only took masses of flak, plus a fine, but I had to officially declare that I withdrew all my suspicions and that Muster was a clean athlete. No evidence has ever been presented that suggests Thomas Muster did anything illegal, and therefore we need to recognise that he was an incredibly fit and dedicated athlete who was an inspiration to everyone who saw him play, especially given the horrendous knee injury he recovered from.

I came away from Monte Carlo scarred from the victory that got away, and scarred from the betrayal of that confidence. But I'd proved that I was competitive again. Muster was literally unbeatable on clay that year, he didn't lose a match on clay until well after the French Open, and I felt that if I could challenge Muster on clay, I could challenge anyone on any surface. I lost to Adrian Voinea in the third round in Paris, but got to the semis at Queen's, and then reached the final at Wimbledon. That made me the first man since tennis went 'open' in 1968 to reach Wimbledon finals 10 years apart. I felt I was really back on top of the world tennis-wise.

To get to the Wimbledon final I had to come through two very big matches. In the quarter-finals I needed a 9-7 final set to beat Cédric Pioline, and then in the semis I came up against Agassi, who was reborn that year. He'd started the year by cutting off his trademark long hair, he was US and Australian Open champion, and he'd got to No. 1... And when he led me 6-1, 4-1 with two breaks in the second set, he must have thought he had me.

There were a lot of sideshows around that match. My coach at the time was Nick Bollettieri. Nick had come to prominence coaching Agassi, but Agassi had split from him about 18 months earlier. Agassi was dating Brooke Shields, who was in the players' box and was celebrating way too early and way too loud. I was mentally very strong then, physically a little tired after the Pioline five-setter, but in good form and feeling good. And yet I couldn't find a way to challenge the Agassi return. There was a bit of friction between Nick and Andre following their split, and I knew a few things about Andre that I wouldn't have known without Nick. Nick had told me before the match that I was doing Andre a favour when I came to the net behind all my serves, especially on his backhand because he had the best backhand return in the world. For a while I was too proud, I said to myself 'This is Boris Becker on grass, I go to the net against everybody.' Well after 6-1 and two breaks in the second, I looked up at Nick, smiled and said to myself 'You know what Nick, I think you may be right. I'm going to stay back now,' and that completely threw Andre off guard.

I've mentioned that I reached the final 10 years after my first final at Wimbledon. Well there was a remarkable parallel with the semi-finals that got me to both finals. What I did to Agassi was exactly what I did to Anders Järryd in the semi-final of 1985 (see page 80). I was outplayed in the first set, but then half-way through the second I stayed back after nearly every second serve, I started to rally with them, and it threw both of them. Playing on grass is about imposing your game on your opponent – if I could impose my game by charging into the net after my second serve, then great, but if I was playing to my opponent's strength, then you have to change your tactics. Staying back robs the returner of the chance to pass the volleyer, and the change worked a treat in both the Järryd and the Agassi matches. Agassi couldn't believe it. I got the two breaks back and won the second set on the tiebreaker, I won the third and fourth, and I beat him from the back. That was one of my biggest wins ever, because at 6-1, 4-1 down it was a joke. There was obviously a bit of a rivalry between Andre and me – not just because of Nick Bollettieri but also because we had different lifestyles and different images. It was definitely one of my greatest victories.

In the final, I took the first set against Sampras on the tiebreak, before he ground me down in four sets. I lost to the better player, there was nothing I could do, but I was very proud of my performance. In those days only the winner did a lap of honour, but as Sampras showed off his trophy, the crowd shouted for me to do a lap of honour with the runner-up's salver – it's now quite common, but I think I was the first one to do the loser's lap of honour. I certainly felt like a winner that day. I felt I was back where I belonged, challenging for the title, and playing one of the all-time greats. I felt very redeemed afterwards. It was a match of very short rallies – I was told later that the longest rally was six strokes. That was tennis at that time. Rightly Wimbledon has changed the grass a bit, and they've slowed down the balls. The Ivanišević- Samparas final in 1998 was worse still, so I think the All England Club's organisers made a change for the better. It was hurting the quality of play, and it affected the audience. Tennis was suffering because of this high-paced superpower tennis. We now have more rallies on grass, which is good, but does that mean you can only win Wimbledon from the baseline? I don't think it does.

Right: **I was down and out against Andre Agassi in the 1995 Wimbledon semi-finals but came back to win.**

Since the start of 2014, Roger Federer has shown that you can win by serving and volleying – you just have to know how to do it. Because he's so talented, I don't think there's anything that Roger can't do on the tennis court. He's simply realising now that his best chance of winning is by coming to the net and playing like nobody else does, because it takes them out of their comfort zone. Since he won Wimbledon from the back of the court, and then Rafa came along and did the same, there's a belief that that's the only way to win, but if you're good enough to serve and volley, and your volleys are good enough, you can still win Grand Slams. Novak has the talent for the volley, he just hasn't put himself into the position to use his volleys a lot, but that might change. Same with Rafa – he has great volleys, he's just never needed to use them. Tennis doesn't want finals without rallies, but nor does it want matches without volleys.

Here's a bit of advice for tennis players at any level, especially a decent level: don't play if you're on antibiotics. I did, and it ended in disaster and heartbreak. In fact it thwarted my last realistic chance of winning a fourth Wimbledon title.

After my defeat to Sampras in 1995, I had a reasonable year, peaking at the right times. I was a semi-finalist at the US Open, losing to Agassi, and I won the ATP World Championship, which was being played for the last time in Frankfurt. I then won the Australian Open, my sixth and final Grand Slam title. The fortnight in Melbourne was a lesson in never judging a player by his form in the first week of a major. I had to go to five sets to beat Greg Rusedski in the first round, and was then two sets down to Thomas Johansson in the second round. In fact I was very lucky in the Johansson match – he had a break point early in the third set, I hit a backhand that was probably out, but it was given in (there was no Hawk-Eye then) and I got

***Left:* But despite my winning the first set, Sampras was just too good for me in the final.**

away with it. That proved the turning point, and I only dropped two more sets in my remaining five matches. Sometimes the top players start a Slam badly, but if they have a moment when their game suddenly clicks, it can be like letting the genie out of the bottle. Both my Australian Open titles had a moment in the first week where I went from being a player struggling to play anything like my best tennis to being a genuine title challenger – against Camporese in 1991 and Johansson in 1996.

After winning the Australian Open, I was fourth in the rankings, and knocking on the door of the world No. 1. I was Wimbledon runner-up, US Open semi-finalist, ATP World Champion and Australian Open champion. Unfortunately I had a bad clay season, but getting back on the grass brought my form back. I won Queen's beating three quality grass courters in the last three matches: Pat Rafter, Wayne Ferreira and my old rival Stefan Edberg in the final. Stefan had announced he was retiring at the end of the year, so the match had something nostalgic about it, but I won, and it left me one of the favourites for Wimbledon. In fact the seeding committee promoted me from my ranking of fourth to being the No. 2 seed behind Sampras, who had won the last three titles. In other words, I was No. 2 seed 12 years after my first main draw Wimbledon, and I felt everything was coming full circle.

It did come full circle, but not in the way I intended. The player who left on crutches on the middle Saturday of 1984 left with torn ligaments in his right wrist on the middle Saturday of 1996. It was the worst possible injury for a right-handed tennis player, and I went from genuine Wimbledon hopeful to thoughts of retirement.

Right: Another trophy on German soil - I finished 1995 by winning the ATP World Championship, played that year for the first time in Hannover.

At the start of the tournament I felt as good at Wimbledon as I had done since 1991. My draw wasn't particularly difficult – the only player I really feared was Sampras, and he had to win six matches before I'd play him. It appeared to be my golden chance of winning my fourth title. I won my second round match on Thursday, but I was feeling a bit weak that night, and I woke up on Friday morning with flu. We had a chat within my team – there was no match on Sunday and on Saturday I was due to play Neville Godwin, a qualifier from South Africa ranked 223. I decided to risk antibiotics, the thinking being that if I could survive Saturday, I'd be back to normal on Monday.

But antibiotics weaken all parts of the body – my reactions, my joints, my ligaments, everything. The first set against Godwin went with serve until 6-6. On the first point of the tiebreaker, he hit a body serve, I wanted to hit a forehand, I was too late, it caught a part of my racket that bent my wrist back, and two of my tendons snapped. And that was that. I tried playing one more point, but realised it was hopeless and shook his hand as gently as I could.

One late move with a weakened body, and the No. 2 seed at Wimbledon, a player challenging for the No. 1 ranking, was on his way to a hospital in Munich with a severe question mark hanging over the rest of his career. While I was in hospital, I watched in frustration as Sampras went out in the quarter-finals, beaten by Richard Krajicek in what was his only defeat at Wimbledon in eight years. I felt the door was open, but I wasn't around to go through it. I watched the Sampras-Krajicek match on television and thought 'S**t'. And the final was between Krajicek and MaliVai Washington, two players who had never played in a Grand Slam final before and never played another after. What a missed opportunity!

I was lucky to have a very nice distraction to stop me from feeling too sorry for myself. During the first week of Wimbledon, the Euro '96 football championships, which were taking place in England, were reaching their climax. I was very close to the German team; in fact I was so close they took me into their bus from the hotel to the stadium. I was even in their locker room, which normally no-one other than the team members and staff get into, but the coach Berti Vogts, the captain Lothar Matthäus and the players Jürgen Klinsmann and Rudi Völler said 'Listen, you're one of us, come with us, you can give us some inspiration'. So I stayed another few days, my doctors were their doctors, they did the MRI on my wrist, put a cast on it (which in retrospect wasn't a wise thing to do – they were probably thinking football, not tennis) – I was fully entrenched in the football squad. It meant that a day after my injury at Wimbledon, I was with the German team in the locker room of the old Wembley Stadium, as 'we' prepared to play the Czech Republic. So when Oliver Bierhoff won the title with the first golden goal to win a major championship, I was very much part of the set-up, even if I had my cast on.

It was a golden moment, because I love football, but coming back to Munich soon brought me down to earth. My doctors made it clear that this could be career-threatening. I was suddenly confronted with the thought of life after tennis.

***Right:* Never play top-level tennis on antibiotics! I did, and it cost me dear at Wimbledon in 1996.**

FABER
lotto
FABER
lotto

Chapter 7

Retirement, twice (1997–99)

'A proper goodbye.'

I was off for more than two months following the wrist injury at Wimbledon. That's when I seriously contemplated stopping. It was good to think about it when I still had a choice, because I decided I didn't want to retire with an injury. I'd come all the way back to be seeded No. 2 at Wimbledon, within striking distance of No. 1 in the rankings – that wasn't the way to go out. But what was? That's when I began to think about my exit strategy. Noah was by then two and a half, Kindergarten was starting, I didn't want to be a dad who was travelling the whole time, dragging him to Melbourne and New York when all he wanted to do was play, so I wanted to make a smart decision about when I'd retire. I discussed it only with Barbara, no-one else. She said it was my decision, but obviously it affected us all.

I had a good autumn. I won Vienna, I won Stuttgart beating Sampras in five sets, and then I lost to Sampras in five in the final of the ATP World Championship in Hannover – that was the third of the three greatest matches I ever played, and the one I lost. By then I was already thanking God or my lucky stars that I'd got back. So I made a promise to myself – I'm sometimes like that – that having worked my way back to the top, I wanted to finish at the top. At the end of 1996 I made the decision that the following year's Wimbledon would be my last. But I wasn't going to tell anyone about it. Not even Barbara knew for certain.

Left: **Pete Sampras was the first to know of my impending retirement during Wimbledon in 1997.**

In my life, it's not easy to keep things to myself. Somehow they leak out, but I didn't tell anyone, not even those closest to me. Barbara and I kept that secret totally to ourselves, and even Barbara wasn't totally sure I meant it, because I think I said I was playing with the idea of this being my last Wimbledon – in my mind I was certain, but I wanted to see her reaction.

I had a pretty good first half of 1997, but psychologically it was Wimbledon, Wimbledon, Wimbledon. I made the quarter-finals to set up a match against Sampras, and of course that was on Centre Court. I felt this was the right moment, the right court, the right venue. So when he beat me in four sets, we shook hands at the net and I told him first. He had a look of disbelief and shock. I knew what I was going to say – all the world saw was that we chatted for a little longer at the net over the handshake than players normally do. Unfortunately the microphones were on, so the media heard it. So when I went to the press conference afterwards there was a murmur, and everyone wanted to know what I'd said to Pete at the net, and whether they had heard right. I said to them that I was happy to make this short – and yes, this was my last match at Wimbledon.

There was silence, disbelief. I explained that with my injury, this was the right place – Sampras is the new owner of the key to Centre Court. I explained I'd play no more Slams, but I'd play the year out and then take it from there. It was such a powerful drug I was on I couldn't just stop overnight. I wanted to slow down my schedule, and I had some unbelievable contracts with some of the tournaments, so I wanted to ease out until the end of 1998, when I'd finish playing for good.

Planning for the future is one thing, but the reality can sometimes be a bigger challenge than you think. It's a common theme with ex-athletes that they struggle with their private lives after they finish competing, because they have so much more time on their hands, including much more time with their partners or wives, and that's something nobody is used to. And how do you deal with that, how do you find a new motivation, a new goal, a new business challenge that gets you as excited as your playing career did? I started a sports management company bearing my name, so I actually went to the office every day, Monday to Friday, during weeks when I wasn't playing a tournament. So that was my routine and I liked it very much. I was home every night. That started after Wimbledon in 1997 when I started preparing my life for after my playing career. But while I had a sense of a new rhythm, not every member of my family liked that. It was more exciting to be in Paris, or London, or New York than to be in Munich every week of the year and travel only to our summer holiday. I enjoyed being home, not having to travel every week, but I don't think Barbara liked it very much.

I had a pretty clear business plan and plenty of business interests; I'd also set up the Mercedes junior squad with six

***Right:* Still serving and volleying in my final appearance at Wimbledon, but Pat Rafter was just too good for me.**

lotto
lotto

promising players and was the Davis Cup supremo, which meant being captain but with a wider brief – so I had a clear idea of what I'd do afterwards as a coach, mentor and businessman. You can't just stop and do nothing. I was still playing doubles in Davis Cup, so it gave me an incentive to play singles. I even got to a clay court final in Gstaad. I was very relaxed on court, I was freaking players out by coming to the net and giving a big kick on my second serve; I had fun and played a style nobody wanted to face. But somehow it wasn't satisfying.

I missed Wimbledon in 1998, and it felt seriously weird. My schedule dictated that I was always in London in June, so it was odd to be in Munich watching it on television. I watched the final in Gstaad as I prepared for the tournament there. I couldn't articulate it yet, but something was still left undone, and I couldn't just pretend that it wasn't important. So at the end of 1998, I spoke to my team and we decided that we'd announce I'd play Wimbledon once more in 1999 but that would be the last tournament – after that, it would be complete retirement as a player. It was the right decision, and it was a relief. I felt I owed it to myself, to my fans, and to the sport to say a proper goodbye.

By early April, things were going well. I reached the final in Hong Kong where it took Agassi to stop me, and I won a round in Monte Carlo. But then at the end of April I was playing football – my hitting partner tackled me, and I broke my ankle so badly that it looked like I'd be out for two months. My injury specialist Hans-Wilhelm Müller Wohlfahrt said 'Listen Boris, you're not going to make it to Wimbledon.' I told him 'Sorry, but I must. There's absolutely no way I'm not playing Wimbledon now.' Well he knows me, and he knew he had to try, so we agreed to do what I could.

It meant I couldn't play any matches up to the grass court season. I tried at Queen's and won a match against Petr Korda, but I was still in pain. Then in the practice week before Wimbledon I hit with Sampras and I had to stop because it hurt me so badly. I went back to Munich and said to Müller Wohlfahrt 'Listen, whatever you have by way of painkillers or needles, give me the strongest within the legal limits.' So I had a cortisone injection. I hardly ever took painkillers or other drugs, I fully respected that tennis is an Olympic sport and I wanted to stay clean. But I wanted the maximum of what was allowed. Müller Wohlfahrt warned me about the after-effects, but I told him there would be no after-effects because after Wimbledon I would stop playing and would then have surgery on the ankle again.

I turned up at Wimbledon hopelessly short of match practice and not knowing if my ankle would hold up, but willing to give it a try. I had a pretty tough draw, but the first round was supposed to be easy. I had a British wildcard Miles Maclagan in the first round, out on No. 2 Court, the scene of so many of my best wins. And there I was: two sets down. I won the third, but he had three match points in the fourth set. If he'd taken one of those match points, my life might have been very different, but I came through it and won fairly easily in the fifth set. I had played terribly. I moved really badly because I hadn't played much before, so I told myself that I just had to accept it.

And yet, it was the same story – I had come through the difficult match and suddenly the wind was in my sails. My second round match was a juicy one for the German media, because I came up against Nicolas Kiefer. He'd been in my Mercedes junior squad, he was the new German No. 1, and the German press was saying I had no chance because I'd barely got through the first round. But even in the twilight of my career I felt I was better than most players on grass, and I beat him in straight sets. Nobody could believe it – including me! But clearly the Maclagan match had got the rust out of my system, and I had the last laugh.

***Left:* By the late 1990s the Wimbledon baselines were starting to get very dusty as serve-volleying began to go out of fashion.**

I then played Lleyton Hewitt, a future No. 1 and a very good grass court player, but not the finished article at that time. Again everyone was saying there's no way I'd beat him. It was a featured Saturday match, and I thought to myself 'Wouldn't it be great to be in the second week of Wimbledon!' I beat him in straight sets.

That set me up for a fourth round match against Pat Rafter, who had won the last two US Opens and was at the top of his form. We were supposed to play on Monday, but there was rain on Sunday and Monday, which gave me time to think 'What if… what if?' To be honest I had too much time to think, and the devil in me came out. Having won three matches I was supposed to lose, I was starting to allow myself to wonder just how far I might go. So in a way I'm grateful to Rafter for having taught me a nice grass court lesson.

He beat me 6-3, 6-2, 6-3, and it was so comprehensive that in the middle of the match I felt 'Yes, it's the right time to move on. I don't have it any more. It's Centre Court, it's Rafter, one of the best players in the world, probably the best volleyer. It's a good way to finish.' I had a nice standing ovation, he walked out first to leave me with the chance to wave to the crowd for the last time, I had a long press conference, and I had a long session with the German media. It was a proper goodbye – the way I always envisioned going out.

What happened that night, the day of my defeat to Rafter, has been well documented, and it doesn't help anyone for me to repeat the facts here, except to say that, thanks to a combination of bizarre circumstances, I ended up having a brief affair with a woman I met at a restaurant in London. Her name was Angela Ermakova, and nine months later our daughter Anna was born.

It hastened the end of my marriage to Barbara. That might have happened anyway as we were having our problems, but while the media had a field day with the story, I gained a daughter, a wonderful young woman I have loved from the day she was born and continue to love now. Of course I was embarrassed and very sad about how it happened, and about the way it broke up my family. It left Anna's mother and me having to set about being parents without any relationship of our own to fall back on. But there are many people who can never have a child, so I really appreciate all my four children. Anna is my only daughter, so while that night in the restaurant was not exactly a model of family planning, I cannot look back on it as a terrible mistake.

It has been hard for Anna. Too much has been said in public about her, she's now 15, and she deserves her peace and privacy. I'm now at a place with her and her mother that's very comfortable, peaceful and family-like. They live about half-an-hour from my home in another district of London. I don't see Anna as much as I'd like, but her mother and I are working on becoming a normal separated family, which hasn't been easy considering our starting point. We've had our battles, we come from different family backgrounds, we have different values and we have different views about education, but I respect very much the fact that she is my daughter's mother. None of us is perfect, I'm certainly not, but the bottom line is that she and I have both matured, and she is very different today than she was 10–15 years ago. Anna is very well educated, she's a good student in a school that stretches her, she's a healthy, young, teenage girl, and that's largely the result of her mother's upbringing. I think we've both become smarter about what we say and do, more so than in the past. Obviously the whole situation was very emotional, and we both said things and did things that in retrospect we perhaps shouldn't have done, but all three of us are moving on in peace and harmony.

Right: **My final farewell - Rafter left the court alone so I could wave goodbye at the end of my final match at Wimbledon, 1999.**

1999

So what else was going on in the world in 1999, the year I ended my playing career at Wimbledon?

The European currency (euro) was launched, even if it didn't become everyday money until 2002. I feel this was one of the biggest lies we were told. We were told the value would be the same, so what used to be two Deutschmarks for something would be one euro, but it quickly became two euros. I'm not saying I'm not a fan of the euro, but the story was told differently to how it's been in reality. I think it was a very clever way by the government to get more value out of money. We had a vote on it, and I voted in favour, but it was sold to us in a way that hasn't proved to be true.

Perhaps the biggest event in retrospect was the Nato bombing of Belgrade. I remember thinking this was the whole of Europe against one small country – it can't be right; it's not fair (I always like a bit of fair play). Among those sheltering from the bombardment was an 11-year-old Novak Djokovic who spent the first fortnight of the bombing in the basement of his grandfather's apartment. I hope we never experience anything like that again.

I had a tiny role in the year's biggest sporting drama. In the European Champions League final, Bayern Munich led Manchester United 1-0 after 90 minutes. There were two people there ready to present the trophy: I would do it if Bayern won, and there was someone else if Man United won. So I was sitting in the stands with Franz Beckenbauer and the head of Uefa Lennart Johansson. As the fourth official showed three minutes of injury time, we left our seats and got into the lift to go down to the pitch to make the presentation. While we were in the lift, Manchester scored two goals in two minutes to win. We came out of the lift, we were almost on the pitch, and suddenly the big screen was showing 2-1 for Man United. I looked at Franz, and he had his hands across his face. I said 'What happened?', and someone said 'We lost', so I couldn't present the trophy.

Among other events that year, Boris Yeltsin and Nelson Mandela (*pictured below*) stepped down as presidents of Russia and South Africa. I met Mandela a few times; he was the most charismatic man I've ever been with. I was at dinners with him five or six times. I never met Yeltsin.

I remember the earthquake in Turkey, which killed more than 15,000 people, because Germany and Turkey are very close due to the number of people of Turkish origin who live in Germany. I was at the Oscars in Los Angeles that year, one of only two times I've been there, and one of the highlights of my year – *Shakespeare in Love* won the best picture award. I did my first advertising campaign for AOL, but the big computer story was that, in the run-up to the year 2000, the world was paranoid about the Y2K Internet bug – it proved to be a false alarm.

And my son Elias was born during the second week of the US Open, so I missed Serena Williams beating Martina Hingis to become the first black woman to win a major title since Althea Gibson 41 years earlier. During my time with Barbara we became good friends with Serena and Venus, and they came to our house a couple of times. (Incidentally, my first son Noah had also been born during a Slam: the Australian Open of 1994.)

Chapter 8

From player to businessman and broadcaster

'Taken seriously in a suit.'

When I retired I became a businessman, but few people know what my business is. I always try to explain that top tennis players are business people. They run a company to manage their name and their brand. Roger Federer is the best example. He has a company, a huge tennis business that uses his name and his distinctive 'RF' logo as its primary brands. Federer is the chairman, chief executive, the major shareholder, the chief financial officer – he's everything, but he has a lot of employees. I know he didn't study at university, but the job made him like that. I was very similar. I had a big turnover as Boris Becker, not only through prize money but endorsement deals and television appearances. The whole business of being Boris Becker was very big, so when I talk about becoming a businessman, I mean that I took a more hands-on role in managing my name and my brand.

To some, that may sound distasteful. It happens to all top players while they're playing, but they don't try to sell it too openly because it doesn't look good for fans around the world. If you think of business and sport, do you play because you can make a lot of money? No, you play because of the competitive instinct, and the money is a nice bonus. It therefore doesn't come across well if we try to market our brands too ostentatiously, so no-one admits to it while they're playing, but that's exactly what it is. Nowadays more than ever players can't admit to it.

It wasn't a big change for me because I'd done it most of my life. But it was a big change for others. People were surprised to see me in a suit rather than tennis shorts. It would look odd if I went into the office in shorts, so I had to dress differently, but I was still the same person with the same philosophy. That's the dilemma a lot of sports stars have when they enter into their second career – the image from the first career is so strong that you can't be taken seriously in a suit or a 9am meeting because people expect you to be on court at three, and that still happens to me today, more than 15 years after my playing career ended. Sportsmen and women have a harder time entering their second career.

Today I run my brand, but I also have a company, Becker Private Office, based in Mayfair, which involves me dealing with finance, private equity.

I've obviously had good years and not-so-good years. I have investments in real estate, the car business, technology, and in social media where I invested little bits in start-up companies. Altogether I have over 200 employees, and I can proudly say that this is a genuine second career following my career as a tennis player.

However, it is a very separate career, one that doesn't seem to the public like a natural follow-on to having been a top-level athlete. I think many tennis fans think that retired players live a life of leisure, getting up after the rest of the world has gone to work, lunching at some tennis club, or waiting for the phone to ring with some invitation to talk about past glories. That is a long way from the way I live now, but it's strange – ironic even – that so many people don't see my business career as something that goes with the Boris Becker brand.

I like to think I understand the value of money. I'm a big spender on my family and friends, though not necessarily on myself. I spend a bit of money on my hobbies. But I have an understanding of money, the importance of it, the necessity of it. After all, I run three families, so I need to understand money.

I'm grateful to tennis for giving me great lessons in that. How to be disciplined, how to be future-oriented, how to take decisions that could affect my family and me, good or bad. So I'm constantly aware of the need to manage life and money. And I love it, I love the fact that I have kids who know that when the house is burning they can call me and I can help them, and that includes their mothers, with whom I have good relationships. I don't think anyone should take that for granted,

***Left:* Flanked by Pat Cash, John McEnroe and Björn Borg, I stand alongside my fellow champions at the Wimbledon Champions Parade in 2000.**

it doesn't happen in every case of broken homes. But I have a patchwork family and I have to act accordingly. My kids deserve that, and therefore their mothers do too, regardless of whether I have conflict with them. And they give me so much back for it, so that's another reason why I like to work, why I like to be busy.

As I've said, I didn't go back to Wimbledon in 1998 after semi-retiring at the 1997 Championships, but there was no staying away the year after my full retirement. In 2000 I was asked to come back for the millennium parade of champions – and I wasn't going to miss that. All the living champions came back, including Björn Borg who was back at Wimbledon for the first time since his last final in 1981. It was one of the most amazing afternoons, and thankfully there's a photo. But I wasn't involved in any other way, and I wasn't living in London, so I came for the ceremony and then flew home.

In 2001 I still needed a sense of separation so didn't come to Wimbledon, but then in 2002 I was asked if I would commentate for the BBC. I felt honoured. German is my first language, English only my second, but I liked the work, and in my first year I was asked to join the team for the final, which is very nerve-wracking. I obviously passed the audition, as I did every men's singles final from then on until 2013. I felt very respected and welcomed, and that built another sense of relationship with Wimbledon.

I was in the news for a couple of years around that time for reasons I wouldn't want. The break-up of my marriage, the subsequent divorce, the furore around Anna's birth, and a horrific lawsuit in which the German tax authorities tried to have me jailed because in the early 1990s I had spent a few nights a year in my sister's flat in Munich when I had notified them that my sole residence was in Monaco. I got off with a fine and a suspended sentence, but the enormity of the lawsuit was brought home when I was refused entry to the USA to see my boys for Christmas because I was branded a criminal. It was an inhumane experience that I never want to go through again.

I think I was so much in the news that people got a bit tired of me, and nobody took the time to see what really happened to me. I also think there was a bit of jealousy. Most people going through a difficult court case, going through a divorce, going through a child born out of wedlock, would have their backs to the wall, but I did pretty well to keep my spirits up and maintain my sense of self, considering what I had to go through. I think that's another reason why people who don't wish me well seize on this time. It's like they can't believe it – like they're saying 'When is this guy falling down? Everyone falls down sometimes. Why isn't he like us?' And my answer was 'Well I was never like anyone else, I am myself, I am Boris Becker.'

I suppose that added to a sense that was developing: that I wasn't totally comfortable with Germany any more. I was living in Zurich at the time, which is German-speaking and less than an hour from the German border, but as I tried to work out where the next stage of my life was taking me, I found little irritations about Germany became bigger irritations.

The German media tries to portray an image of me to the German people that's really old and long gone, and not representative of who I am today or have been in the last few years. The recognition as the youngest-ever Wimbledon champion – I was often referred to in Germany as 'der siebzehnjährige Leimener', the 17-year-old from Leimen, long after I'd ceased to be 17 or live in Leimen – was so strong that a lot of journalists who like me and respect me don't really understand how I moved away from tennis after my playing days. It started with the language: my professional language today is English and it was 10 years ago. Most German journalists don't speak English that well so they don't understand why I'm popular in England, what I'm saying, why people think I'm funny, because they don't understand the humour. And because of this non-understanding they became critical, implying I'm no longer one of them.

I – and everyone who's been with me over the past 10 years – am flabbergasted at how I'm portrayed in some parts of the German media. It's like a completely different person to who I am today and who I've been in recent years. And that creates a problem, because obviously I have a pretty good name in Germany, I have contractual obligations, I have private and business matters, but I spend so much of my time explaining that I'm not the man I'm painted as in the media. I often find myself chatting to people who, after a while, are surprised to realise who I am today compared with what they read in most publications, which is very frustrating at times.

Left: The international dimension to my family has been enhanced by marriage to Lilly, my second wife who is Dutch of German and Surinamese parentage.

Let's be honest: there are far more important things in this world than Boris Becker. But I think a lot of people who make comments about me haven't given themselves time to think about me, and what I've done. They therefore put me into boxes: Boris Becker – tennis player, youngest-ever Wimbledon champion, tennis commentator-cum-businessman, but nobody's taken the time to think about or read about what I've *really* achieved. So when you don't see me for a while, a lot of people think I stay in bed all day, or I wait for something to happen, or I'm playing X-Box, or watching tennis, or whatever. I don't mind if they don't know much about me, but I do resent it when people talk about me without knowing who I am or what I'm doing.

The next stage in my relationship with Wimbledon began to take shape in September 2005, on the sixth birthday of my son Elias.

I was in Miami, and we were celebrating Elias's birthday with him, Noah and their mother. At about 9pm, Noah wanted some pizza, so we went to my local Italian, Sylvano's on Miami Beach. There were a group of young women sitting in the restaurant, and my eye was drawn to one of them. I like to think I have a qualified eye for spotting talent, and I immediately saw the talent. I was standing at the bar with Noah, and she came to the counter to order something. I have to admit I was a little bit struck by lightning. I'm not usually short of words, but I was on this occasion, so I asked Noah to start the conversation for me. Noah was 11. He muttered the first words 'How are you?', she answered him, and I kept prompting him, telling him what to say. Eventually she looked at me, and I took over.

We just chatted for a few minutes – she told me she was a model from the Netherlands working in Miami – but then she went back to her friends. From the way she had ordered her drink, it was clear she was friends with the woman behind the bar, so I asked her if I could have her name and number. It took me about an hour to get it, but she said her name was Sharlely Kerssenberg, known as Lilly, and gave me her number.

That was 4 September. At that time I was living a couple of months of the year in Miami to be close to my sons. I tried calling her for literally two and a half months, first in English, then in German, then in my very limited Dutch, using every language I knew. I left dozens of messages on her voicemail, but she never responded. Being a bit of a macho man and expecting every girl to respond to me when I call, I was very intrigued by this stubbornness and this unwillingness to connect with me. I thought 'What have I done? Speak to me!'

By chance I saw her about three months after our original meeting, only quickly, but she was with a girlfriend, so I asked the girlfriend if she could find a way to get Lilly back to the restaurant as I really wanted to chat with her. The friend got her there at 11 o'clock one night, and that's when we started talking properly for the first time. It was only 10–15 minutes on a Saturday night and she was very glamorously dressed to go to a party on the beach. So I asked if she wanted to meet for tea on Monday afternoon. Just stop and think about this: tea in the afternoon? We're talking Miami Beach here – nobody drinks tea, it's too hot. I don't even drink tea! I don't know why I came up with that idea – maybe it sounded innocent, it was a safe time of day and you can meet for tea in half-an-hour so if you don't click in that time you can handle a wasted half-hour. Whatever my reason, I left her with my number, but she didn't call back. I therefore assumed she wasn't interested so on the Monday I played golf with Sylvano, the owner of the Italian restaurant.

At three o'clock she called me, saying 'Where are you? Didn't we want to go for tea today?' I said I couldn't do tea, but asked if she would like to do dinner that night? We met for dinner at Sylvano's at 9pm, but she arrived at 9:45pm, so for half-an-hour I was convinced she wasn't going to come. When she eventually arrived she looked beautiful and sexy, and that's when we properly sat down and found chatting was easy. Three hours flew by, and at 1am I wanted to do the gentlemanly thing and drive her home. She told me she lived in the Murano Grande. At first I didn't take it in, because that's where I lived. It turned out she lived on the fifth floor of the same apartment building where I had the penthouse. So I drove her home, it wasn't far, and I wanted to give her a peck on the cheek. But she said 'No, no', turned me round and kissed me full on the lips. So the macho man wants to be the gentleman, but the lady goes straight for the lips! I have to say I was a little surprised by that, but I admired her for it.

And that was that. We saw each other next day for lunch, and we started our relationship that week. That went on for about two years. And then I said 'Listen, I want to go to the next step, I want to take you to my home, and I want you to meet my mother.' So she flew with me for the first time to Zurich, and we drove to my mother's in Leimen. Lilly can speak a little German – her mother was from Surinam, and her father was German so she was able to relate to my mother.

Like Barbara and my boys, Lilly is mixed-race, but she didn't really know her parents as both were killed in a car crash when she was very young. That has left her with a strong sense of family, and her sense of what we're building is even stronger

Above: **Lilly has really embraced all my children - pictured here with Noah, Elias and me during Wimbledon fortnight.**

than mine. In our living room we have a piece of Lilly's artwork, which includes the text:

In this house we do REAL
We do mistakes
We do I'm sorry
We do second chances
We do fun
We do hugs
We do forgiveness
We do really loud
We do family
We do love
We are family!

What attracted me most was her ability to connect with all of my kids. That was her biggest quality, and I think that's her core. She never had her own family. Maybe she fell in love with Noah at Sylvano's and had to marry his dad! Or maybe she fell in love with all of us because we're a family, and that's very important to her.

It was important to me that Noah and Elias were comfortable with their dad having a new girlfriend. I'd been single for almost 10 years. Noah had known a couple of my girlfriends in between, but when he saw I was getting serious with Lilly, we had a father and son discussion. I asked him if he liked her. He said he obviously loved his mother, but added about Lilly 'she's the best one you've had since. I like her a lot, and she's cool with us, so if you want to marry her you have my blessing.'

In December 2008 we had a skiing holiday in St Moritz: Noah, Elias, Lilly and I. It was such a beautiful holiday. On 30 December I asked Lilly if she would marry me. We married in St Moritz six months later. Elias helped in finding our engagement rings. St Moritz is not that big, and in the Badrutt's Palace there's a beautiful Cartier store which I walked past every day, so I signalled to him what I liked, and he got them.

There was then the question about where we would live. Lilly was pregnant and we had to decide where we wanted to have the baby and raise it. Lilly had a flat in London, my daughter lives in London, and I had two or three weeks of work per year at Wimbledon. I was living in Zurich at the time, but Lilly and I have spoken English since we first met, and all my children go to English or American schools, so we agreed to live in London. London is big, and it didn't have to be Wimbledon. But my history with the All England Club drew me towards Wimbledon, and things naturally fell into place. I like the lifestyle, I like the village feel despite being close to one of the biggest cities in the world, we have proper parks, and there are elements of country living despite being so close to the city. It has always seemed a good place to raise a family.

At the time of writing this, we've been in Wimbledon over five years. Lilly and I have had our ups and downs, as all couples do, but I feel our little family is part of a bigger patchwork family that's largely intact. There are many situations when all my kids speak with Lilly behind my back, perhaps when I've done something wrong or if I'm moody, so they talk to each other about how they can 'relax Dad'. That's Lilly's biggest quality: her ability to understand the importance of my older kids to me, and the guilt I feel that I'm no longer with their mother. I know things happen, that in this day and age unfortunately 50 per cent of marriages go wrong, for whatever reason, but we have kids, and I'm a strong believer that we have our responsibilities as parents, and we have to find a way to include all members in any new family structure. Sometimes it's very difficult, to the point of being impossible, but we should always try to find a way. It's not the kids' fault that parents get divorced, whatever explanation every parent has.

My wife and ex-wife often speak on the phone, about holidays, birthdays, parties, presents. I appreciate that and don't

***Right:* I'm not just a tennis player - I enjoy the sand too!**

BARCLAYS
CYCLE HIRE
FILA
BARCLAYS
10383

take it for granted – I can't force that to happen but it's nice that it does. Both women are mature enough to understand that it's just part of the deal. And Noah and Elias have a younger brother – we don't say 'half-brother', we say 'brother'. They also have a sister, not a 'half-sister' but a 'sister'. We've never managed to get all four of them together. The three older ones have had holidays together in Majorca, but we're yet to get all four together in one place. It's one of my goals for the near future to find a situation where all four can be together for the first time. I don't want to force it, everyone has to be cool with it, but it's obviously my wish.

Amadeus was born in London in March 2010. We are applying for him to have British citizenship, just to confirm that we can call this home. My daughter Anna and her mother Angela both have British citizenship. And that then raises the question about me.

The longer I live in London, the more I have a longing for British citizenship. Obviously it has professional implications, especially if you have business interests in the UK, and having been raised a proud German and won the Davis Cup and Olympic gold for Germany, it would be a wrench. But I wouldn't rule it out. That decision is for later, but the fact that we are applying for citizenship for Amadeus means we're all thinking about it.

The discussion about British citizenship throws into question my relationship with Germany, which is a strange one these days. It starts with the language – I get the sense that a lot of Germans don't even think I'm German. I even get German tourists or German people abroad speaking English to me. I hear their accent, and I say to them, 'If you want to speak German, I'm happy to do so.' They almost seem confused about whether I'm English or German. It's unfortunate, but a lot starts and ends with the language. I spend about three-quarters of the day speaking English. I like to think my English is OK – it's not perfect, but it's OK. I got the sense that Germany accepted me being in Switzerland, because it's a German-speaking country, but there's a bit of history between England and Germany. It's as if the Germans are uncomfortable that I'm so popular in England, as if the English shouldn't like Boris Becker because he's 'one of us'.

I was also somewhat hurt by the reaction in the German media when the news broke that I was to be Novak Djokovic's head coach. Some of the German media were genuinely asking whether I understood tennis, and whether I'd have the qualifications, knowledge and understanding to work with a player as good as Djokovic. That's how ridiculous it became. It would have been legitimate to ask whether I was able to put across my knowledge in a way that would have been useful to Novak, but in Germany it went further than that. It was literally 'does he understand tennis enough to help a player of Djokovic's calibre?' It was also interesting at the end of 2014 to see how many stories there were in the German media about Djokovic as 'the comeback kid' – the subtext to this was a fair bit of face-saving on the part of journalists who had questioned my suitability for the job. I wasn't trying to prove people wrong, they had simply been wrong to question it in the first place.

I should point out that much of the issue to do with my relationship with Germany has to do with the media, not the people. I don't dislike Germany, I'm still comfortable in my native tongue; I can speak and dream in German, even though I dream mostly in English. Most of the German public like me, or certainly respect me – they don't always understand me, but even if all they see of me is on a television game show in a nice suit, I think most people take the view 'What's there not to like?'

The problem is that the name 'Boris Becker' sells a lot of headlines if there's a scandal involved and if there's no scandal involved they have to create one or not write about me. Since

***Left:* I love London - they even have Boris Bikes for hire!**

I've matured and lived quietly, my private life doesn't sell newspapers. That's the problem they have with me – it's either huge news or no news. I sometimes say to people that in most countries I'm a sports star, but in Germany I'm a phenomenon, and it's very difficult to be a normal person when you're a phenomenon. I was recently at Munich airport, collecting my bags, when a member of the German public recognised me and started talking to me. He said 'But you're picking up your own suitcase!' I said of course I was picking up my own suitcase, why shouldn't I? He said 'Well I expected you to have an army of minders who do that for you.' That's obviously the image many people have of me. Some superstars may have that, but it's not me. This is how the false and outdated media image of Boris Becker continues, but it's not who I am. All I want is to be given a fair chance to be who I am, but it seems impossible in Germany, at least for the moment.

This is why I don't think I'll ever live in Germany again. I stress it's nothing against the country; it's simply for reasons of privacy. Maybe as I get older, people will stop prying and my relationship with Germany and the German media will naturally get better – only time will tell. I think it's important to also say that my feeling of being at home in England doesn't mean I'm turning my back on Germany or becoming in some way un-German. If Germany plays England at football, I still want Germany to win, but I want England to come second. I cheer for both Germany and England, but if they meet in the final I want the Germans to win. I represented Germany for 15 years, they played the anthem for me, I won the Olympic gold medal and the Davis Cup for Germany, so it would be lying and not true to my core if I said I didn't instinctively want Germany to win. My feeling of being at home in England and possibly applying for British citizenship won't change that.

Right: **I support many charities. Here I am playing football in Port-Au-Prince for the Haiti Laureus Football Project.**

FIFA

I don't spend much time in Germany any more. When I go there to appear on a game show or other entertainment programme, a few people question whether my German will be good enough because they only hear me in English these days. It sounds ridiculous, but it's true. We're back to the problem that I've moved on with my life, but the German media haven't. When I first won Wimbledon at 17, my language skills weren't as good as they are now – it's hardly surprising, which 17-year-old has those skills when faced with the world's media? But that was 30 years ago, and many of these people haven't adjusted their focus. It's frustrating for me, and very disrespectful, not just to me but to athletes in general because it implies that because I never took my 'Abitur' (the German equivalent of A'-Levels or baccalaureate) and only concentrated on sports, I can't be very intelligent. I sense this really applies more to Germany than anywhere else.

Although I find it disrespectful, maybe I'm a challenge to the Germans' belief that you can't make it without decent academic qualifications. Not only did I do well without my Abitur, but to make matters worse I became immensely popular. A lot of kids looked at me and thought that if I could do it at 17, they could too. In that respect, I've been subversive because I've shown you can be successful without the educational qualifications. People are frightened about that in Germany.

Another problem in Germany is that tennis is broadcast less frequently on TV than it was 20 years ago. It means they don't see me – British TV viewers see more of me because they show more tennis and I spent more than 10 years on the BBC. Other German athletes suffer from that too. Football is so dominant in Germany that German sports fans miss out on some beautiful sporting moments in other sports, with the result that many German athletes are internationally successful without the German people knowing it because it's not televised. I don't think that's right or fair.

There's still the question of racism. I like to think I helped Germany become more tolerant – I certainly set an example. But because of economic factors, extremism is coming back into Germany, whether it's the far right or left, and I think that's a dangerous phenomenon. My lifestyle and my opinions don't help there. On the contrary, they see me as an outsider. The German people think 'He's not one of us any more, he was married to a mixed-race or coloured girl, he has mixed-race children, he lives in England', so in many ways I've moved away from my German heritage. Whether that ends up in a British passport is another question, but it all contributes to my feeling of being more at home in England.

Furthermore my relationship with England is good. I live in the British capital. I say to my German friends that I like to live in 'peace and freedom', and I really feel that living in London is about that. Everyone has their bit of freedom and democracy, and it's really up to you whether you make it in this city, and therefore in this country, or whether you don't. There's a freedom of choice in so many ways, and I think that really fits my character and my family. I hope I can stay here for the rest of my life.

Right: **Tennis and politics is an interesting mix. I've played with a number of high-profile people since retiring, including David Cameron.**

Chapter 9

Returning as a coach (2013–14)

'The most emotional I've been since I stopped playing.'

I came full circle with Wimbledon in 2014. Thirty years after walking into the ground for my first main draw tournament as a player, I walked in as the head coach of one of the front-line favourites for the title. I was used to walking through the gates of the All England Club, but I hadn't played tennis at Wimbledon for many years, I hadn't been to the practice courts, and it was odd not to be wearing a suit but tennis clothing. But I had a mission – to see Novak Djokovic to a second Wimbledon title.

My appointment in November 2013 as Novak's new head coach had been a big story. In short, people were shocked that he had asked me. I was obviously surprised about some of the reactions. If there's one area where nobody should doubt my knowledge, it's tennis. We can't disagree that my eyes are blue – even if you don't like me, my eyes are still blue. So by the same measure, even if you don't like me you still have to respect my knowledge about the sport. But that's the world we live in. We live in times of a very powerful media. Social media is partly responsible for that, but written media is too. Headlines, for instance are important – without headlines you don't make the story – but headlines don't make the truth, they're just selling points.

I understood that some people wondered whether I could put my knowledge across to Novak in a way that would help him play better. After all, I had never coached a top-level player. But people were dismissing me because I'd been 'just a commentator'. As a commentator, I may be sitting and talking about tennis, but I still have to provide some substance. When you commentate on a Wimbledon final, you can't just joke around. You have to be serious, or the broadcaster – the BBC in my case – won't let you commentate again. You have to come up with some kind of information that's new, accurate and valid. In fact my work as a commentator allowed me to help Novak, because I hadn't been away from the game. I was in the first row when Djokovic lost to Murray in the Wimbledon final in 2013; I was in the first row when Djokovic lost to Nadal in the French Open final in 2012, so these matches weren't something I'd read about in the papers. I could see first-hand the mistakes he was making, and I think that's something people didn't think about.

As for Wimbledon, I actually played on the courts for 15 years before commenting for 12 years, so if there's one guy who should know a little about it, it's me. I think maybe my image as a successful player was too big and the change from player to commentator was too much for some people to handle; then having got used to me as a commentator, the change to coach was also quite large and they had a hard time putting it together.

It all began in October 2013. I was in Johannesburg at 'One Young World', a conference organised by Bob Geldof and Kofi Annan which brings together the most important entrepreneurs aged 25 or under from 180 countries. There we talk about politics, economics, and things like the social importance of sports. I speak about subjects that are important and affect my

***Right:* My personal relationship with Novak really blossomed during Wimbledon 2014.**

UNI
QLO

life. While I was there, I got a call from Novak's manager, Edoardo Artaldi, who I've known for years. It was the Saturday of the China Open; the day Novak lost his No. 1 ranking after Nadal had won the first semi-final in Beijing. Edoardo said 'Could you imagine becoming coach of Novak?' I thanked him for the consideration, said I was honoured and felt very humble, and suggested we meet to discuss it. We met in Monte Carlo about a week and a half later, and I asked him what I could bring to the table. That was exactly the question everyone else asked afterwards. We had a full-on 24-hour discussion about what Novak thought he was lacking, what he thought I could help him with, and I agreed. I said I thought that I had qualities which, when matched with his situation, could improve his tennis, but I had to be sure. If I get into something, I don't do it half-heartedly; if I'm going to be away from my family for long periods, I have to know it's worth it, and I don't mean financially – I have to know it's worth the effort to put my heart and soul out there.

In the course of October and November we had a constant dialogue about matches, scheduling, attitude, all sorts of things. I felt there was a real commitment on Novak's part about working with me. Then I started talking with Marian Vajda, his head coach of the previous eight years who wanted to travel less. We spoke about some of the things I see in Novak's game that I wanted to change, and we began a conversation about how to make Novak a better tennis player. I felt there was a real challenge, and I wanted to get involved. Finally it was agreed that I would join the team, but in effect I was already working with him in Paris, London and the Davis Cup final, and he didn't lose a match for the rest of the year. In fact it went so well from the start that Novak even invited me to sit with his team at the O2 in London, but I felt that was the wrong start.

The question then was how we would announce it. We came out with the statement soon after the Davis Cup final, I joined him for a training camp in Marbella, and then I went with him to Abu Dhabi and Melbourne.

The reaction of the tennis world was largely one of shock and puzzlement, and as I've said, at times strayed into being insulting and disrespectful. I understand the questions about why Novak needs anyone, and whether I'm the right man, but look at the situation. For a start, he lost the No. 1 ranking to Nadal after losing a couple of big matches, and he was smart enough to recognise that his game was sliding. We can see that now, but he saw it at the time. Because of that intelligence and instinct, he wanted to get advice from somebody who could help him stop the slide and hopefully make him better, and he chose me. He's not stupid – if it turned out that I'm not the right man, we would have parted company. But the idea that appointing me was some kind of fashion statement because Murray had hired Lendl, Federer had hired Edberg, Čilić had hired Ivanišević and so on underestimates both him and me.

I really want to emphasise that this is a team effort, and has been from the first day of my involvement. I may have the title of 'head coach', but I couldn't do the job without Marian Vajda. Before every match in 2014, whether he was at the tournament or I was, we spoke at length. We spoke before every match in Melbourne and every match at Wimbledon, because I would be stupid not to use the expertise of someone who has been with Novak for some time. That also goes for his physio, his conditioning trainer and his manager, all of whom have been there for a long time. I may be the biggest cheese, but I'm still just part of the team. A few people have chosen to compare Marian and me – but that's nonsense! I bring something to the table that Marian doesn't have, and Marian brings something I don't have. I think the combination is perfect.

Not that the media saw all this, which very much clouded the way they reported on our first six months working together.

***Left:* 'You're not going to break an egg with that serve...' I look on as Novak serves at the Australian Open.**

UNI
QLO

The Australian Open in Melbourne was perhaps the worst possible tournament to begin the coaching partnership. Novak had won the competition three times in a row, so anything less than winning a fourth consecutive title would be a let-down. And that's what it looked like to the world. He lost to Stan Wawrinka in the quarter-finals, but players know when they get lucky or unlucky. Novak understood that he'd got lucky the previous year when he beat Stan 12-10 in the fifth, and this time he got unlucky and lost 9-7 in the fifth. That happens – there are days when all your big shots hit the lines, and there are days when they all just miss the lines, and it's nothing to do with good or bad coaching. In hindsight, the trip to Australia was the best thing for us. It gave us three or four weeks to get to know each other better in the midst of the nitty-gritty and the pressure. Despite losing in the quarters, the time in Australia gave us a good start.

Then in February, when I joined him in Dubai, Novak found out that his girlfriend Jelena was pregnant, so he wasn't really concentrating on tennis or practising, he was celebrating the fact that he was to become a father. It was an impossible tournament, but I happened to be there. We knew that, but the world didn't because he wasn't going to tell everyone about the pregnancy so early.

Then I messed up my hip and had to have an operation, so I couldn't go to Indian Wells and Miami. Marian therefore agreed to be with Novak for those two tournaments, but I was in constant contact with Marian – we spoke before every match. Again the media didn't know that and when Novak won both tournaments, the headline was that Djokovic wins when Becker is absent. Again it's important what the player and coaches know, and much less important how it looks to the world outside.

***Left:* With Novak I'm part of a team that includes Marian Vajda, his physio Milan Amanovic, and his manager Edoardo Artaldi.**

I was back with him in Monte Carlo, where he injured his arm and lost to Federer in the semi-finals. It wasn't *exactly* my fault, but the media pointed out that the only two tournaments he had won by mid-May were the two where I was absent.

Finally the whole team was back together in Rome, and Novak beat Nadal in the final. That was very important for Novak's peace of mind – having Marian and me there; the way he won the tournament gave him a lot of confidence, and the belief that he was with the right team. It doesn't matter who's on site and who's at home – it's working. We were then all together at the French, which was a great tournament. Reaching the French Open final is a tremendous achievement for any player, and losing to Nadal in Paris is no disgrace.

But then the spotlight falls on me. Next up is Wimbledon, and now I have to deliver, because that's my territory, I know grass court tennis better than most. And I'm alone – I talk to Marian regularly, but I'm on my own in arranging practice sessions and strategy. Finally after the match point in the final, in his mind and my mind and everyone's mind, it has worked. If he'd lost, say against Čilić in the quarter-finals when he was really struggling or to Federer in the final, it wouldn't have been the end of the world, but it might have put doubts his mind and mine. I might have thought that maybe I couldn't help him; that I was trying to get him to be something he isn't. Sport is defined by winning and losing. The margins may be fine, but there's a difference, and it was very important for us that Wimbledon ended in triumph.

So Wimbledon was the most important tournament for our relationship. By a mixture of good luck and good management, I managed to combine what I knew about the place and playing on grass, and use the fact that it is my home to deepen the relationship I have with Novak.

Walking through the gates was a bit of a weird situation for me. I'd lived in the village, played in the qualifying, been champion three times, commentated on the final for more than 10 years, sat in the Royal Box – and here I was entering the grounds in a totally different role. Especially the week before, that was surreal. Novak and his physio had to remind me about the white clothing rule. I don't think I'd even played at the Aorangi Park practice courts since my last year as a player in 1999.

It was a very personal affair. This is my home, and I wanted to protect my home. The week before, I showed Novak and his team a few things in Wimbledon village and in London, things they didn't know, parks to go to, local things that you only know if you live in Wimbledon. For example, the traffic is different on Tuesdays compared with Wednesdays, and there are certain times of day that are best for going into central London. Most of the time we were seeing London, I was driving him – usually he has a driver, but on this occasion I was the chauffeur, and he was surprised and impressed with my local knowledge.

The World Cup was on, so we went to San Lorenzo in Wimbledon. In my playing days I used to go to the San Lorenzo Italian restaurant in Beauchamp Place, Kensington, but since then, the owner's two sons have opened up a second San Lorenzo in Wimbledon, so we went there to eat and watch a couple of matches. Novak came to my home too. I have evenings here during Wimbledon when a few of my friends drop in; in fact every other night in 2014 we had an interesting group of people. Lilly does a very good chicken, so one night we had John and Patrick McEnroe over for the USA v Belgium match. The same evening Novak and Jelena were out walking their dog, and they happened to knock at the door and said 'Can we come in?' I said of course. Novak thought it was unbelievable to find John McEnroe sitting there watching the football. 'This is home,' I said, 'I live here! These are my friends.' I was very pleased that Novak and Jelena felt comfortable knocking at my

Right: **The WTA's Kids in the Park Mini Tennis at Wimbledon is a great opportunity for players of all ages to play on courts near my home.**

PUMA

door and popping in. We ended up having chicken, watching America play, and we took a picture of three Wimbledon champions in my hall. It just happened spontaneously. When you see the picture, you understand the vibe – just three guys sharing the same experience.

I said I wanted to protect my home. I mean that, both in the sense of the house and village, and also the All England Club. I wanted to protect my memories of the locker room and being a player. But during the two weeks of the Championships I know every little thing there, and I saw my role as turning that into something of value for Novak.

After his tough loss against Nadal at the French Open two weeks earlier, I saw it as my job to pick him up, and to make him understand that this was different now. We practised on the lower courts at Aorangi, which are terrible. They're really bad, but when he asked me why we were practising there, I told him he needed to practise there to understand Centre Court better – if you think there's a bad bounce on Centre Court, practise on the lower courts and then you'll find there are no more bad bounces on Centre. I found a few journeymen players to practise with him, and he often asked me why I was using certain people – I told him they had things that could help him, like a good serve or a good return, so just accept it. These are things I wouldn't do at the French or the US Open, but I do at Wimbledon because I know the place.

We had a scare on the first Friday. He beat Gilles Simon, but he fell on his hand at the end, and that was a frightening moment. He had an MRI scan and found there was nothing wrong. Then Novak asked what we were planning to do Saturday and Sunday, and I said, 'Saturday you don't play. There's enough time. You want to win next Sunday, not this Sunday, so you take a day off and rest your mind as well as

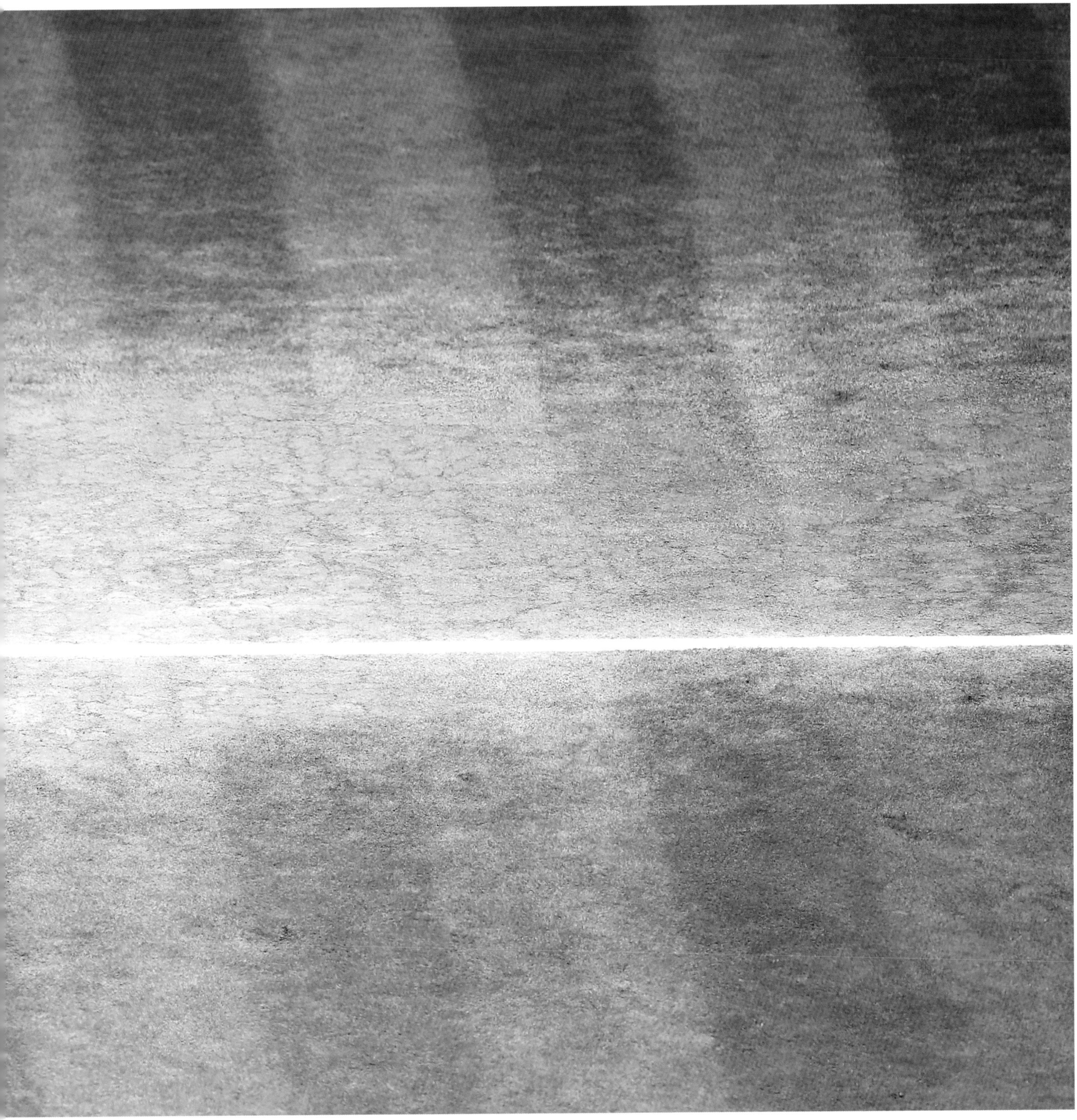

your body. On Sunday you can have a good practice session.' Things like that may make a difference in the end. It was my responsibility, and he trusted me.

In the second week, he played unbelievably against Jo-Wilfried Tsonga, but on Wednesday against Marin Čilić he was struggling. Čilić had taken a set off him at the French, and looked to be getting closer. Novak was two-sets-to-one down, and was playing on No. 1 Court for the first time. He came through it in five sets, but it was a close thing. The next day, the Thursday, Novak asked me to come to the house he was renting in Wimbledon, and we had a long, three-hour conversation over dinner: Jelena, his brother Marko, Novak and me. It was after that conversation that I felt I really belonged in the inner circle of Novak Djokovic. He asked me questions about preparation, about Wimbledon, and many personal things. We were sitting at the kitchen table, and talked about very personal stuff. Jelena is a very important part of his life, and this was the week before they were due to get married. I just said what I felt. Afterwards, Novak said the time spent with me during dinner altered his perspective towards me. He also made a conscious effort to invite Lilly and me to their wedding. I knew when the wedding was, I had been invited three months earlier, but I felt it was a polite invitation to a very private, small, family wedding with no celebrities. But that evening he made it clear he really wanted Lilly and me to be there. So I felt our relationship went to a new level that night.

The 2014 final against Roger Federer was one of the great matches, but from my perspective the words that come to mind to describe that day are 'surreal' and 'eerie'. It was also strange in the sense that it was almost a film script – the two modern-day heroes out on court, and the old rivals Edberg and Becker sitting on either side of the Players' Box.

***Left:* An incredibly emotional moment! It was wonderful to be part of a team effort that saw Novak win Wimbledon in 2014.**

PUGEOT

There were a lot of familiar moments in the hours leading up to the match. I knew exactly what to do, where to go, how to be in the best frame of mind for the final – so many things that I had done as a player, rehearsed in my mind and was now doing as a coach. It's not like football where each team has a separate locker room – there's one main locker room, and both players are in it. I remember from my three finals with Edberg that we were together in that locker room, going through our preparation, and here we were as coaches to the rival players in the final. Novak, I and other members of his team all assembled in the locker room at about 1:30pm, half an hour before he was due to walk on court, to have our final group session. At that point, Federer and Edberg got up and left – I don't know where they went, but they obviously felt their privacy was compromised so they went somewhere else. I felt a sense of 15-love, that we'd struck the first blow. It was an eerie, tense moment, but a telling one.

Novak led 5-2 in the fourth set and had a match point, but Roger saved it and took the match into a fifth. At that stage Novak wisely took a bathroom break, something we had discussed in case he got into that situation. It just allowed him to regroup. We knew Roger would be strong, and at one stage in the fifth set he looked the likelier winner. But they both know that the margins are fine, and on this occasion Novak came through it.

I think the end of the match was the most emotional I've been since I stopped playing. There's a picture, a selfie that I took with some of Novak's team in the Players' Box. It's wonderful to have that photo and to have been part of a Wimbledon triumph in a different way. As we left the Players' Box and went to link up with Novak in the main clubhouse building, Edberg and Federer came up and congratulated me – they were both very gracious and gentlemanly. And then Rod Laver walked in, someone who has to be in anyone's top three greatest players of all time. Which meant for a few moments we had Laver, Federer, Djokovic, Edberg and me all together. And that night at the Champions' Dinner, I got to touch the Wimbledon men's singles trophy for the first time in 25 years, which was another very moving moment. I had truly come full circle.

***Left:* Once my trophy, now in the hands of the man I coach.**

I feel that over the time we've been working together, Novak has re-established himself as the dominant player in tennis, and I'd like to think I've had a small role in that. It doesn't mean he's going to win every match he plays, or every Grand Slam final. But if his critics are honest, they've seen him play over the first year I've been coaching him, and there were changes in his game plan and his positioning, maybe on his serve, maybe in the way he has finished matches, that he hasn't done for a while. Looking back at my career, you always have to reinvent yourself as a player because the locker room doesn't sleep – players read your weaknesses, and you have to play better this year than you did last year in order just to hold your place, let alone improve. As a player I did that, and all the top players have done it. The list is long of players who have what they call 'super coaches', but it speaks for the intelligence of the player to understand that, if they want to continue being in the top five, they have to answer new questions that they're asked on a tennis court. And Novak happened to ask me to help him.

It means being back on the road for 25 weeks of the year, including a month in Australia in the European winter and a month in America in the summer (it's not all glitz and glamour, trust me!). One of the reasons I stopped playing was that I couldn't take all the travelling, but I think I'm doing it again for the right cause, and as long as I feel I can help Novak, as long as I feel there are elements of his game I can still help him improve, I want to be part of the team. Of course he also has to agree that I'm still the right person. It's a proper partnership, made up of him understanding what he needs and me being able to give it.

My perfect scenario would always be to have Marian at every tournament, and I've told him that, but I understand he can't travel as much as he used to. On the other hand I can't be at every tournament, so I'm at the Masters and the majors.

There was a joke put about that Novak had only hired me because he wanted to brush up on his German. We do speak German sometimes, particularly when the locker room is full. When I have to say something important I choose to speak in English. My Serbian is very limited, apart from the swear words! Novak is talented with languages – he hears one and picks it up. His German was surprisingly good when I first spoke to him, and it's got better. He now has the chance to improve his German by speaking it with me, while I have the chance to develop a world-class player after coaching plenty of juniors and up-and-coming players. You see, we both benefit!

Working with one player means I can no longer do my work for the BBC as a commentator and pundit. It's a shame, but I quite understand the deal. People still ask me about the greatest players, in fact they probably ask me more now because I have the inside track on the top player of this era.

The best player I ever played against was Pete Sampras. He definitely had the best serve I've ever faced, and he was the best all-round player. He's the reason I stopped believing I could win Wimbledon any more. Even his so-called weakness, his backhand, was good enough to set up the rest of his game. It was good enough to return and keep the ball solidly enough in play, and his movement was so good you often couldn't get to the backhand as much as you wanted to.

People ask me whether Federer would have beaten Sampras. They only played once and Federer won, but Sampras was past his best by then. What you have to remember is that tennis starts with the only shot that doesn't depend on your opponent, namely your serve, and I consider Pete Sampras's the best serve of all time. Players always have trouble against his serve because they just can't get the ball back, and then the pressure is higher if they have to hold their serve knowing that one break for their opponent means the set has gone. That's something very few people understand. Federer is by far the most successful tennis player of all time, counted in Grand Slams, and Jimmy Connors won more singles titles and matches over five sets. But if they played Sampras at his peak, would they have been able to get his serve back often enough to win? I doubt it.

People often ask me who the greatest player of all time is. I respond by saying it's not fair to compare generations. I never played Laver, but the guy won two calendar-year Grand Slams, and he was the only player to win the Grand Slam when everybody was eligible to play, so that puts his performance into the right light. To say that he wasn't as good as Federer would not be fair. How do you rate Borg? Winning Wimbledon from the back of the court five years running? – they said you couldn't do that, but he did it five times, mostly after winning the French Open just before. That's a feat that Federer has done once and Nadal twice, but Borg did it three times! Yes, Nadal is impossible to play at the French Open, but how about Borg v Nadal with the same rackets? I sometimes discuss this with Novak – there were great tennis players before, and there are going to be great players in the future, so it's very unfair to all the good ones to say who is better. People used to play with wooden rackets; now they have the products of high-tech research and development. Travelling was far more difficult then; now they travel in private jets – we forget that flying economy class was an improvement on travelling by boat, which often took a few days or more. We mustn't knock the top players of the past just because we know more about the top players of today.

Right: **Pete Sampras – perhaps the greatest player of all time.**

FABER
lotto
lotto
FABER
lotto

There's an idea that tennis is more competitive these days, that more people have the chance to play, and today's top players play to a higher standard than past generations. I'm not sure about this. If it's so easy to do, why does the Lawn Tennis Association (LTA) struggle to find a 10-year-old British kid who's good enough to be the next Andy Murray? The LTA isn't short of money. If it's so easy to do, why hasn't the German federation found a world-beater since the era of me, Stich and Graf? If it's so easy, why hasn't the American federation found another McEnroe?

The fact is it's not about money. It is about knowledge, the eye of the beholder, and who's in charge of the junior programme. Are they looking to spot a character that can handle the pressure in a Wimbledon final, or are they looking to spot a nice forehand that comes from a wealthy family? I'll let you judge what they're looking for. The best player in the world today comes from a war-torn country and he was not blessed with wealthy parents, there was no tennis background, and he didn't have the means to travel the world as a junior. The most successful player of all time comes from a pretty wealthy background in one of the safest places in the world, Switzerland. My point is that it doesn't matter where you come from – it's about your character, your personality, your drive, your motivation, and finding the right people at the right time to better your professional life. I think it speaks for the intelligence of Federer and Djokovic that they did the right things at the right time to become better tennis players. Novak moved to Germany at 14 because he had run out of options in Belgrade to become a better tennis player. Roger didn't have to do that because there were enough indoor tennis facilities in Basel and nearby, but he picked the right coaches. I think Peter Lundgren was very important for Federer's development, and so were Jelena Gencic and Niki Pilić for the development of Djokovic. Federer and Djokovic also found ways to broaden their horizons, and then take the necessary steps: staying in Basel, going to Munich, and so forth. Andy Murray moved to Spain when he was 15 because he thought it would improve his game, and he was right. What I'm saying is that it's very difficult to say what's the right way, but having lots of money doesn't mean you'll find it.

The strength of competition today is a big debate. If you look at the Slams over the past 10 years, from the 2005 French Open to the 2013 US Open, we had just five different singles winners in 35 Slams, 32 of them shared between Federer, Nadal and Djokovic. Is that because those three were so much better than the rest, or weren't the rest good enough? You can make the case for either argument. In every era before, you had multiple Grand Slam winners, but why? Because the No. 1 wasn't as good, or because there was greater competition among the top players? Again I leave that open for judgement. It's just that I hesitate to say that McEnroe wasn't as good on grass as Federer, even though Federer won seven Wimbledon titles to McEnroe's three. I played McEnroe, and he was a genius, but I still say Sampras was better because you couldn't touch his serve. McEnroe's serve was good and his volleys were very good, but you could play against them, whereas Sampras had such a good serve you couldn't even start the rally because you couldn't get the ball back. And even when you could, he was so agile, he could hit the big forehand, he was great at the net – so what could you do? The chances are you'd lose 7-6, 6-4 every time.

In fairness, the game has changed since then, and perhaps that's something we don't mention enough. There was a time when Ivanišević, Krajicek and Sampras dominated Wimbledon with their big serves, and that was boring. So they had to slow down the game. The organisers at Wimbledon swear the grass is the same, but I think the grass is a little thicker now. Certainly the balls are softer, and therefore slower.

***Left:* McEnroe was an absolute genius on the court.**

Some people still ask me how fast I serve. Well my fastest serve was 239 kilometres an hour, which is faster than most guys serve today, but I wasn't the fastest server – Rusedski, Krajicek, Ivanišević all had bigger serves. It was tough to win in those days because against some guys you just couldn't return. On the other hand, I've never seen anybody as flexible on the tennis court as Djokovic, and I'm not just saying this because I coach him now. I've never seen anybody who can slide on a hard court, move his knees and ankles, and get into situations to play a shot where most other players would break their leg or their ankle. Novak's strength and flexibility and balance are by far the best of everybody. His mobility and balance make up his biggest weapon, so he can still play passing shots when he's out of position. I think his background in skiing helps, but he also works very hard.

The best returner I ever played against was Andre Agassi. He was even better than Jimmy Connors. Unfortunately I never played Novak, but he looks awfully close. When he's on and he's returning the Milos Raonic serve, for example, his timing is mind-boggling, especially on the backhand return. I don't understand how you can do that against the best servers today.

I think the biggest difference today is the racket technology. Players have better and faster rackets. The equipment allows more freedom, especially three or four feet behind the baseline.

In terms of fitness, I think players today work more off the court. I have a hard time saying they're fitter because I don't think Borg was unfit, nor Năstase, nor me. Today's top players pay more attention to nutrition; they pay more attention to medical advice; they have more of a proper tennis regime. Players of my generation played more tennis, in particular more doubles. It's more scientific nowadays, therefore the quality of training is probably higher, but does it make for better tennis? It makes for better tennis if Federer, Nadal or Djokovic are at their peak and they play five hours in Melbourne, or if Federer and Djokovic play a classic five-set Wimbledon final like they did in 2014. But I don't think the Borg-McEnroe Wimbledon final in 1980 was bad. To compare is often impossible, but I love to debate about it, and I love to debate with Novak. He agrees with me that it was a different era and a different generation back then, so comparisons are hard, and nobody can prove who was better. It's a good point for talk shows, but you shouldn't disrespect people. It goes for other sports too: is Messi better than Maradona, is Neymar better than Pele, is Schweisteiger better than Beckenbauer? I don't know, because I *can't* know. Towards the end of 2014, I was approached by Chris Kermode, the chief executive of the ATP, and asked if I would sit on an advisory body of ex-players whose job would be to make recommendations about how top-level tennis could be improved. Nothing is off-limits; we are free to think the unthinkable. The other members of the group are John McEnroe, Mats Wilander, Lleyton Hewitt and Carlos Moya – all five of us Grand Slam singles champions and former No. 1s. At the time of writing this, we have yet to meet as a group of five (Lleyton was absent when the other four of us met in London in November 2014), but the kind of things I want us to discuss include possible rule and calendar changes.

I think the time taken between points needs to be standardised between the Grand Slams and the tour events. It's crazy to have 20 seconds in one and 25 seconds in the other, with one group enforcing it more rigidly than the other. There's also the question of whether a player is entitled to be tipped off by an umpire before being given a warning for a time violation. Some players take the mickey all the time, but I believe players have to be informed that they are breaking the rule. It would be great to speed up the game, but we need to keep the discretion with the umpire, so that when you have Nadal and Djokovic having a 50-stoke rally, you can allow them longer after that point. To have players going to the towel after every point on a cool day is wrong.

***Right:* Andre Agassi was the best returner I ever played against.**

Another area we could look at is the warm-up – is it too long, should it stay in its current format? I also want us to look at the player's code of conduct, in the hope that we can find ways to allow players to express themselves more on court. Then the real personalities can come out more, and the fans can engage with the players as people and not just as tennis players.

The world doesn't know enough about the players outside Djokovic, Federer, Nadal and Murray. That's a mistake that starts with the players and their agents, and their understanding of what branding and exposure mean. More exposure means more income. There are more fascinating personalities on the tour, but players and their agents don't understand about getting exposure for them. That becomes a problem for tennis, because once Federer stops playing, or once Nadal is too injured to play, who's going to be the next big thing, or the rival to Djokovic that everyone wants to watch? If the next big rivalry is Djokovic and Nishikori, that's great for Europe and Asia, but without getting Nishikori better known it's a disaster for America. It's not the players' fault, it's their advisers', and the ATP has to advise players on the need to spend longer with journalists and express their views about whatever they feel strongly about. The players and the sport will benefit from it.

It will also get rid of a bit of the dishonesty about the image of tennis – the idea that the players are all friends. It's very difficult for a top player to have a genuine friendship with a competitor. In fact I don't think nowadays the top 10 are friends. They respect each other, and it's good that they set standards of good behaviour so youngsters get the message that you have to respect your opponents. But don't be fooled by how much they hug each other after matches – that's partly staged, it looks good, but I don't think it's truthful. In my days my Davis Cup teammates were friends, although I must admit that was because I felt they weren't real rivals and I could tell them at night what I was going through, without them being good enough to take advantage of it on court. I would never spill my beans to Edberg, to Wilander, to Lendl, to McEnroe. As I've said, Michael Stich and I were never friends, and when we played in the same Davis Cup team in 1995 we kept it very businesslike. I therefore hope that through the ATP advisory board I can contribute to tennis fans seeing a bit more of the top players' personalities, so we enjoy real rivalries – respectful rivalries, for sure, but without the pretence that these guys are friends with each other.

Finally we need to take a look at the calendar. The new 'third week' between the French Open and Wimbledon is a good thing since it emphasises the importance of grass court tennis and the opportunity for better preparation can only enhance the prestige of Wimbledon. The Davis Cup obviously needs some attention, but we need to be open-minded about some of the other ideas for promoting tennis. I was involved in the first International Professional Tennis League (IPTL) in Asia in November and December 2014 – both as an ambassador and doing interviews with all the leading players for the official television feed. In many ways the IPTL was a great success, it certainly took the world's top players to parts of the globe they normally never play in, and we need to have a calendar that's open to initiatives like this, rather than treating them as exhibitions that have to find a slot in the few cramped weeks of the off season.

Boris Becker's Wimbledon

If you haven't been to Wimbledon, please pay a visit! You don't have to limit it to the two weeks of the Championships, in fact in some ways Wimbledon is much more manageable outside the tennis fortnight. And when I talk about Wimbledon, I mean both the town and the tennis.

There are two parts of Wimbledon – Wimbledon Broadway and Wimbledon village. The Broadway is at the bottom of the hill, by the railway station. That's where the shopping, some restaurants and the theatre are. Wimbledon village is at the top of Wimbledon Hill, and includes the original village which backs onto Wimbledon common, a lovely area of woodland which you'd never believe is on the edge of one of the world's busiest cities. The village has most of the restaurants and a few boutique shops; the restaurants are a little more user-friendly outside the Championship fortnight because they're less crowded.

The All England Club doesn't really belong to either of these parts. It's an offshoot of the village in a green area between Wimbledon and Southfields. If you come to the All England Club outside the Championships, you can still visit, in fact if you pay to go into the Wimbledon Museum, you can go into Centre Court in a way you couldn't while the tennis is on, unless you have a Centre Court ticket. You can quite legitimately say you've been to the tennis at Wimbledon if you are just visiting London for a weekend in November!

To me, Wimbledon looks like an old cowboy town without horses. I can imagine people riding their horses through the main village many years ago, and it still happens – there's a stable on the common where people take their horses out for walks. It has that feel of a western town where you know the butcher and the postman, and these days you know your Chinese takeaway and your Italian restaurant. You know the people personally, and if you're around for long enough they'll deliver the food to your home. It's the kind of place where, if you don't immediately pay, you say you'll come back next week to pay, and they're fine with it – yes, that still happens in Wimbledon. I know all my neighbours here; we meet once every couple of months for a football match or a night out. It's small-town living, with all its qualities – and its disadvantages, of course – but living close to one of the biggest metropolises in the world has its charm. It feels a little bit like time stood still in Wimbledon.

People will wonder whether my view is coloured by 'famous person syndrome' – whether I find Wimbledon very friendly because people recognise me and want the reflected glory of being seen with a famous person. I'm sure that doesn't work to my disadvantage, but I've lived in Germany and I didn't have that feeling then. I didn't know my neighbours in Munich, even though I lived there for many years in the 1990s, in fact whenever I did something I could be fairly sure I'd read about it in the papers the next day – in a negative way. Here I feel more protected. I think people like me living here; they feel complimented by my choice to live here. I have no idea if it's cool to live near Boris Becker – people tell me I've raised the property prices by living here, which may or may not be true, but I feel people protect me. I can walk through the village and if someone notices me they will say hello and shake my hand, but they won't ask me for photos or autographs, or not often. I think they're almost proud that I've chosen this part of the world as my home, and because of that I think they're quite protective.

The hospitality also extends to the Championship fortnight. It's a place where Novak Djokovic and his wife can walk the dog – the village is full of tennis fans, but nobody stops him. Maybe a few don't recognise him because they simply don't expect him to be out with his wife and the dog, but people living here are used to big stars, so there's a mentality that protects everyone who lives here, and their guests.

Wimbledon offers me everything: a place to call home, access to one of the world's great cities, access to an airport for me to go anywhere in the world I need to, and a local tennis club that reminds me of my greatest achievements. And since Roger Federer started going to the net again, it's also reminded me of the way I used to play. I've said for years that there's still room for serve-and-volley in today's tennis – you just need to know how to do it – and now Federer is proving me right! If ever I get over all my knee and ankle problems, I might even start hitting balls again, and rushing some poor returner by charging into the net behind my serve. Or maybe not.

It's been a long journey. Thirty years ago I didn't know if my gamble to try and make it as a tennis player would work. Then it worked with instant, almost incredible success. The journey since then has been a mixed one, with good things and not-so-good things. I've made mistakes, and I've paid a heavy price for some of them, but show me someone who hasn't made mistakes and I'll show you someone who hasn't lived. I think I know who I am. There are not many things that are great about getting older, but one of them is that you truly get a sense of yourself, your qualities, your failures, your strengths and your weaknesses, and your understanding of your own character. And you deal with it. I'm very comfortable in my own skin.

I thank Wimbledon for its central part in my journey. I sincerely hope that I'll be living in Wimbledon for the rest of my life. I don't know whether that will happen, but that's the plan today. I know this village better than any village in the world, and that includes my hometown where my mother still lives. It is my home.

Index

(the initials BB refer to Boris Becker; page numbers in italic type refer to photographs)

Picture Credits

Courtesy of Brian Holmes: p. 50.
Courtesy of Boris Becker: p. 201.
Courtesy of Getty Images: pp. 10, 11, 12-13, 14, 15, 16-17, 18, 19, 20-21, 22, 24, 24-25, 26-27, 29, 32, 33 left, 33 right, 34-35, 36, 39, 40, 43 left, 43 right, 44-45, 48-49, 51, 52, 55, 56-57, 57, 59, 60-61, 63, 66 above, 66 below, 67, 69, 70, 71, 72, 75, 76, 78, 81, 82, 85, 88-89, 91, 93, 94, 95, 97, 98, 102-103, 105, 108, 110-111, 112, 114, 116, 118-119, 121, 122-123, 125, 126, 127, 128, 131, 132, 135, 141, 142, 145, 147, 148, 151, 153, 155, 156, 157, 159, 162-163, 165, 166, 169, 171, 174, 177, 178, 181, 183, 184, 186-187, 189, 193, 194, 196-197, 199, 200-201, 202-203, 204-205, 206, 209, 210, 213, 215, 218-219, 224.